USER RESEARCH WITH KIDS

HOW TO EFFECTIVELY CONDUCT RESEARCH WITH PARTICIPANTS AGED 3-16

Thomas Visby Snitker

Apress®

User Research with Kids: How to Effectively Conduct Research with Participants Aged 3-16

Thomas Visby Snitker
Nordhavn, Denmark

ISBN-13 (pbk): 978-1-4842-7070-7   ISBN-13 (electronic): 978-1-4842-7071-4
https://doi.org/10.1007/978-1-4842-7071-4

Managing Director, Apress Media LLC: Welmoed Spahr
Acquisitions Editor: Shiva Ramachandran
Development Editor: Matthew Moodie
Coordinating Editor: Nancy Chen, Rita Fernando

Cover designed by eStudioCalamar

Distributed to the book trade worldwide by Springer Science+Business Media New York, 1 New York Plaza, New York, NY 100043. Phone 1-800-SPRINGER, fax (201) 348-4505, e-mail orders-ny@springer-sbm.com, or visit www.springeronline.com. Apress Media, LLC is a California LLC and the sole member (owner) is Springer Science + Business Media Finance Inc (SSBM Finance Inc). SSBM Finance Inc is a **Delaware** corporation.

For information on translations, please e-mail booktranslations@springernature.com; for reprint, paperback, or audio rights, please e-mail bookpermissions@springernature.com.

Apress titles may be purchased in bulk for academic, corporate, or promotional use. eBook versions and licenses are also available for most titles. For more information, reference our Print and eBook Bulk Sales web page at http://www.apress.com/bulk-sales.

Any source code or other supplementary material referenced by the author in this book is available to readers on GitHub via the book's product page, located at www.apress.com/9781484270707. For more detailed information, please visit http://www.apress.com/source-code.

Printed on acid-free paper

Contents

About the Author

Thomas Visby Snitker is Senior User Research Manager at LEGO (The LEGO Agency) and former CEO, owner, and founder of a research company under his own name (2005). Thomas is passionate about user centricity, research, user experience (UX), and usability. He enjoys writing and has contributed two chapters, "User Research Throughout the World" and "The Impact of Culture on User Research," in the *Handbook of Global User Research* (Morgan Kaufman, 2009). He's also published a book titled *Breaking Through to the Other Side: Using User Experience in Web, Interactive TV and Mobile Services.*

Thomas is a frequent speaker at Danish and international conferences, such as the UX Masterclass, and occasionally blogs for the Danish edition of *Computerworld*. In addition, he serves as an external reviewer at the IT University of Copenhagen, the Copenhagen Business School, the Technical University of Denmark, and the Information Science School of Copenhagen.

Before he founded SnitkerGroup, Thomas worked as a usability specialist in IT (in KMD), in a media agency (Mediacom/Beyond Interactive), and a web agency (Signal Digital/GreyDigital).

He is the father of Sigge, Anders, and Peter and lives in Denmark with his wife Katie and their cats. He enjoys the cultural activities that you'd expect from a self-described mainstream cis male born in a previous century – from photography and music to cooking, Wordfeuding, and biking.

Here he is, circa 1972, 2011, and 2017. He will love to hear from you at thomas@snitker.com.

Acknowledgments

Warm thanks to the five practitioners: Camilla Balslev from DR (Denmark's Broadcasting Corporation), Garrett James Jaeger from the LEGO Foundation, Jennifer Wells from CodeSpark, Nanna Borum from LEGO's Creative Play Lab, and Rasmus Horn from LEGO Education.

Huge thanks to Derek Zinger and Gregg Bernstein, Dina Kapengut, Hakan Gonen, Emil Voxby, Stephanie Pedersen, Johanne Kirkeby, Hannah Jensen, Kashmiri Stec, Fylla Fjordside, Jaleh Behravan, Pia Breum Corlin, Peter Birkedal, Rasmus Horn, Nancy Mahmoud, (Super)Nicklas Lind, and Carsten Baagøe Stokholm for tireless reviews and to Esteban Kolsky for feedback.

DISCLAIMER: LEGO, the LEGO logo, the Brick and Knob configurations, and the minifigure are trademarks of the LEGO group, which does not sponsor, authorize, or endorse this book.

Understanding Kids and Their Experiences

An introduction to research with kids

As a designer, producer, marketeer, or researcher with children as the audience, you must be cognizant that kids behave differently than adults in order to be successful. You need to include the kids in the process through all of the stages, from the early ideation phases all the way to conceptualization, design, prototyping, and eventually the launch.

This book aims to inspire practitioners who are working in this development and design process, and can be sometimes overwhelmed with the challenges it poses.

During my years as a research manager in LEGO's internal agency, I have introduced many new colleagues and interns to the ways in which we can involve kids in our research, and every time I have searched for a good book on the subject. Unable to find one, I decided to write this book. I hope you will find it beneficial.

© Thomas Visby Snitker 2021
T. V. Snitker, *User Research with Kids*, https://doi.org/10.1007/978-1-4842-7071-4_1

Adults who research kids' experiences venture into a familiar yet foreign land where the inhabitants speak a different (yet familiar) language; have different norms, values, and goals; and behave and interact differently. The adults will struggle to settle in that land and will likely not be accepted as peers by the kids.

Two important aspects set children and adult researchers apart:

- As an adult, you wield the entire arsenal of adult competence – you understand and control your world, you are sovereign and autonomous, you can think and do and say whatever you want, and you are responsible for your choices and actions. Kids are not.

- When it comes to research, you can be a researcher and a respondent and also a sponsor or stakeholder of research. You adapt your behavior to each of these positions. Kids in most instances cannot and care not.

So research with kids, such as interviewing a child or observing a child interacting with a product or service, is very different from research with adults, and any research must be conceived and executed with the child and the child's world in mind in order to be successful. The researcher needs to understand both worlds and build a bridge between them. This book is about that bridge and how to build it.

Design, innovation, and the need for research – and KX, Kids' Experience

> *The person's interpretation of experience is simultaneously the most significant product of an encounter and the spur to the next.*
>
> —Jerome Kagan, *The Nature of the Child* (Basic Books 1984)

We can understand what causes a person to say, feel, and act the way they do only to the extent that we can access the content of that person's experience. One reliable and scalable way to access kids' experiences is through research, and by studying how they interact with things, how they communicate and behave. This book primarily focuses on kids' experiences with *designed* objects and services. Design is how we invent and reinvent our world; design is how we produce and reproduce the tools, the content, and the services that help us achieve things, but also overcome our inconveniences, fears, and inadequacies, our restlessness and boredom, our curiosity and inquisitiveness.

This definition means that design is not an activity only done by designers (i.e., people with a design degree or the word design in their job title) or only done in an explicit design context, but design is a commonplace activity that most people do at multiple times in their daily work lives and in their private lives alike – they come up with new ways of going about their business and their existence. And increasingly so; as societies develop and new practices and technologies emerge, so does the need to design these, often in an almost Darwinian way; new ideas that actually "survive" the first few months whether on the marketplace or in our culture are surprisingly few. So we probably design much more than we are actually aware of.

A given new idea may have outlived its commercial or practical use, or it may be impossible to implement in society at large or in an organization due to its complexity or external dependencies. In the context of commercial innovation, it is highly valuable to be able to quickly nurture good ideas and turn them into products/services on the marketplace, and thus innovation adds to the competitiveness of the company in many ways. That is, whether the company can find out which ideas of the many ideas generated in the company are actually feasible and whether it can manage the process of quickly discarding bad ideas while keeping the good ones. The potential gain – and this is where research plays a crucial role – is to avoid wasting precious time, personnel, and materials on designing, producing, marketing, and supporting a failed or substandard product or service, for example, one that simply does not meet the needs of the audience. "Getting the right ideas right"[1] – and doing this quicker – means that the company can bring more meaningful and pleasurable products and services to the market faster than the competition.

Since most, if not all, of the design for kids is done by adults, the designing adults need to understand how a kid can use and experience a tool or service. Luckily, we live in a time where UX, User Experience, has grown in influence as an approach that has the intended audience much closer to heart and mind than earlier design and development paradigms. Also, the related approach of CX, Customer Experience, has grown, as it supplements UX with the shopping dimension that is so crucial to all commerce.

However, neither the aspect of being a user nor a customer will teach you much about the kids' experience, so I propose a new term, the KX or Kids' Experience. When accomplishing a task, the *user* or the *customer* has a desired outcome in mind: trying (hard) to reduce errors and waste of resources. This is sometimes called extrinsic motivation.

---

[1]*The Creative Curve: How to Develop the Right Idea, at the Right Time* by Allen Gannett (Currency 2018): www.thecreativecurve.com/ is a good source of inspiration; it documents how creativity can be understood as the result of hard work and a rigorous process (as opposed to inspiration and talent).

But kids are often simply playing, or "goofing around." Their motivation is often intrinsic: it is driven by an interest or enjoyment in the task itself, and the aim is to attain one's own internal rewards. It has little focus on external pressures and little or no desire for consideration. Play helps the child in many ways and is not a waste of time; it develops all kinds of social, cognitive, and physical competencies. The KX is very similar to the UX and the CX in that it is concerned with a *human* experience, but it is special in several ways and requires special attention:

- Kids have different needs than adults.

- Kids have different goals and success criteria than adults.

- Kids have other capabilities than adults.

- Kids follow different user journeys than adults.

- Kids express themselves differently from adults.

Play is a *job to be done*

Another noteworthy innovation and design approach, jobs to be done, may be of inspiration.

The concept of "jobs to be done" was made popular by business leaders Clayton Christensen and Michael Raynor in *The Innovator's Solution* (Harvard Business Review Press 2013), and Jim Kalbach expanded upon it in *The Jobs To Be Done Playbook* (Rosenfeld Media 2020).

It follows a simple principle: people "hire" products and services to get a job done. For instance, you might hire a new bike to make your commute faster or get exercise. Or, you hire an ice cream to reward yourself after hard work.

Play *is* a job to be done in order to develop and grow up, but play is also very different from any job in the sense that play and playing is a goal in itself. An adult may accept to work a job in order to get paid and there's a long list of good reasons why, from self-actualization to supporting a family. These reasons all revolve around an outcome, or, in other words, the reasons are justified by the adult and often by society as a whole. A child may accept to play (to work as a "player," as someone who plays) for a very different set of reasons that don't revolve around outcome or justification. As a designer or innovator this provides a very different set of challenges and opportunities than when adults are your audience. It can be hard to describe to other adults a design that has no outcome or justification in the adult world but has it in abundance in the children's world.

Another aspect of play is that it is performed and desired by the same individual in ways that may vary over the course of just a few months or even days, as the experience of childhood is one of literally constant growth and change. If you are an adult designer or innovator with play and young *players* as your audience, your process needs to be able to focus on the abilities and demands of the individual and simultaneously consider their ongoing developmental process – or risk your product becoming obsolete overnight simply because your audience grew in age. If you design for adults, there's clearly also a constant risk of products becoming irrelevant as the market evolves, develops, or moves on, but it happens at a very different cadence.

To sum up, there are many ways in which conventional wisdom for design and innovation does not work when it comes to kids and play. There are many obvious parallels between the adult experience and the Kids' Experience (KX), but it is important to consider them as distinct worlds and to handle them with two different approaches. I will explain why. Keep reading.

What to expect when you're expecting… kids for research

If you are new to the practice, among the first things you'll notice that is different about research with kids as opposed to research with adults is that the respondents are not their own masters – they can't decide for themselves. Instead, usually a parent or sometimes a school teacher makes decisions on their behalf, including the decision to join a study.

You will likely see a few examples of a misalignment between the child and the adult, for example, that the child wants to join your study but the adults say no, or vice versa, that the adult signs the child up for something they are not actually interested in.

Also, there may be misalignment between child and adult about what will take place during the session. The adult may also be mistaken or out-of-date when it comes to knowing the child's interest, which may lead the adult to sign the child up for a session about something they may no longer be interested in.

Sometimes a parent completely understands your requirements for the research (the where, the when, the how, the why, etc.) and relays this completely to the participating child, but sometimes just partially, and you have no way of knowing which is the case until you have the child in front of you.

The child may be expecting you to do the talking, or that the research session is a play session or a performance test. A lot can go wrong when the child's expectations are not met. It is sometimes tricky enough to get adults who participate in research to fully understand what a given research session is about, and with kids this challenge is, in a way, doubled. One way the researcher may tackle this is to expect nothing in terms of the child's understanding and expectations, and to be ready to introduce everything from the very beginning. This broad-minded approach also oftentimes opens the study up to unexpected insights.

Kids' research and rocket science

In some cases kids' research is not that complicated. If you don't expect to base very important decisions upon it, a small and less-precise study may suffice — it is better to do a minuscule study than no study at all.

A key hurdle for many professionals and students is quite simply to prioritize practical field work over the comfortable office furniture; to them field work requires too much preparation and planning, it takes time, perhaps there are costs, certainly a lot of hassle. Perhaps they prefer to google their way to an insight[2] or to rely on their own personal experiences. Perhaps they work in a context that has little or no tradition of field research — the first step in a new direction being the hardest. Perhaps they are surrounded by very clever people who are more than willing to offer their opinions (and perhaps that's also what they find most interesting about their job) — opinions that, on the one hand, will "spare" everyone the effort of going into the field, but, on the other hand, are not to be confused with facts and the discovery of new insights.

A classic study in 1989[3] by Jakob Nielsen (engineer, author, and early champion of usability testing) concludes that testing with five people lets you find almost as many usability problems as you'd find using many more test participants. As long as it is "... aimed at collecting insights to drive your design, not numbers to impress people in PowerPoint."[4]

It is an interesting article with a striking graph at its center, but it can be a little bit misleading on its own, but it can be complemented[5] with the article "How to find more usability problems with fewer users"[6] by Dr. David Travis of UserFocus. This article dives into the original study behind the graph and the math that points to the fact that "the correct formulation is: '5 participants are enough to get 85% of the usability problems that affect 1 in 3 users,'" which, in short, bridges both the likelihood of discovery (the 85%) and the frequency of problem occurrence (31% on average, so roughly 1 in 3, but likely higher in the prototype phase and lower after the product is launched)[7].

To add to the complexity, one needs to also consider how many test participants are required to find most of the important, the *critical,* problems — and not just insignificant cosmetic problems. Rolf Molich[8], the grand old man

---

[2]Chapter 4 has plenty of examples of this practice. Apparently there *are* things that you simply can't learn from "googling" as this article points to: www.quora.com/What-are-some-things-one-can-not-find-on-Google

[3]With updates in 2000: www.nngroup.com/articles/why-you-only-need-to-test-with-5-users/

[4]The quote being from 2012: www.nngroup.com/articles/how-many-test-users/

[5]Thanks to Emil Voxby, who reviewed this book, for pointing this out.

[6]www.userfocus.co.uk/articles/more-usability-problems-with-fewer-users.html

[7]https://measuringu.com/five-users/#many by Jeff Sauro

[8]www.dialogdesign.dk/about-rolf-molich/

of usability studies, conducted a large number of studies (so-called Comparative User Evaluations, CUE-1 to CUE-10[9], some of which I had the pleasure to participate in) to establish an answer, which is that the number is huge:

> A large number of test participants (>>100) and a large number of moderators (>>30) will be required to find most of the critical problems.

Hence, Molich concludes that

> five users will only find a small fraction of the usability problems in a product (but five users are great to drive an iterative process anyway).[10]

The point is that *small can be good*, and that you should feel empowered to run studies with small sample sizes if that is all your resources, time, and budget allow. In fact, it is sometimes ignored that a small qualitative study (with 5 or 10 respondents) is usually much faster than a large one (with 50 or 100) and that the small study can have a tremendous impact simply by helping and informing quickly, at a time where designers and developers still have time and resources available to adapt to the findings. The recommendation is not to stop testing completely after 5 respondents but to plan for ongoing but smaller tests, rather than one or two larger tests (or no tests at all).

This advantage of research agility is even more pronounced in those earlier phases of a project where numerous and crucial decisions are made – even a small amount of research will have a large impact when it is timed and scoped right. In a business context where the time to market is often crucial, planning for multiple iterative smaller studies rather than one big study in the beginning, middle, or the end (or even worse – no audience studies at all) can be helpful while making better use of resources. I will speculate that this agile approach could work in rocket design too – the agile approach has replaced the waterfall model in many other domains already.

There are many requirements that a research project (whether academic or commercial) must meet in order to be credible and impactful. One is that the researcher must clearly indicate exactly how reliable the study is, for example, keeping the scope and nature of the study out in the open is necessary. It is very important to be explicit about how serious and solid the study is. Basing a decision on research with five respondents is much better than basing it on the opinions of the stakeholders or on a google search where hearsay and myths blend together with serious research.

---

[9]https://interactions.acm.org/archive/view/november-december-2018/are-usability-evaluations-reproducible
[10]www.dialogdesign.dk/cue-studies/

The status of children in research and in society – and in your own mind

If you have experience researching adults and you expect in a research project with children to simply duplicate your effort and approach, just perhaps scaled down in age, you may be in for a few surprises and setbacks.

The main focus of this book is kids' research in the realms of design, innovation, and marketing – realms that are closely linked to the trends in the society at large, be it in sociology, technology, pedagogy, or psychology, to name a few. One cannot work in kids' research without acknowledging a host of factors that affect or govern how children are raised and how they develop.

Samantha Punch is Professor of Sociology, Social Policy, and Criminology at the University of Stirling. Her PhD included two years of ethnographic fieldwork on rural childhood in Bolivia, exploring children's daily lives at work, home, play, and school. In *Research with Children: The Same or Different from Research with Adults?*[11], she taps into central discussions in society and academia that are still pertinent.

One is *the competence and status of children*, which is also central to research. The following extract from her article highlights the very central dilemma we face as adult researchers, as she examines the tendency to perceive research with children as one of two extremes: either exactly the same as, or entirely different from, adults. As a researcher it is important to align the choice of research method with the status of children:

> If children are perceived as "the same as adults," the researcher will not come up with a special "kid sized" protocol but instead try to treat them as any other person, whether grown-up or not. This approach may skirt over the blatant differences between a child and an adult.

> If on the other hand children are perceived as "different from adults," the researcher will need to come up with ways to describe or at least understand this difference and how it can manifest itself in a study. Ethnography – immersing oneself into a culture and adapting its norms and behaviours – is often considered the most valid approach to bridge this gap. But this approach needs to accept the fact that adults cannot be children – not the children they themselves once were and not the same as those who are now children.

---

[11] "Research with Children: The Same or Different from Research with Adults?" Punch, Samantha, in *Childhood: A Global Journal of Child Research*, 2002, Vol.9(3), p.321

Punch also highlights how the core relationship between adults and children affects research.

Most children are used to having much – if not all – of their lives dominated by adults (from soft-touch guidance to heavy-handed imperatives), so children tend to expect adults' power over them and they are not used to being treated as equals by adults. In this respect children are marginalized in adult-centred society, since they do not experience equal power relations with adults and much in their lives is controlled and limited by adults.

As an adult researcher, clearly you were once a child and thus in one theoretical dimension you are an expert on childhood. But in another dimension, your childhood occurred in a different time period, maybe in a different place, likely with different values, certainly with different technologies available. So the context was very different. And then (and this is a third dimension) you, the adult researcher, grew up, learned new things, forgot about things that are no longer acceptable or relevant, so you, in essence, cannot return to your childhood self. As a researcher you must recognize these three dimensions and realize how, and to what extent, this influences your relationships with your child respondents and your research.

Instead of seeking (perhaps unconsciously) to replicate a study setup that is designed for research with adults, the researcher will increase the likelihood of a successful study by expecting different social norms and ways of expression in the kids' study. The metaphor of two different worlds, the kids' and the adults', may be helpful in this context to remind you as a researcher that either you accept the biases of studying kids in an adult world (the research project) or you accept the biases of trying to enter the kids' world with your study. In most cases there will be a middle ground between these two theoretical positions, and you can take any number of steps specific to your project that will create a shared space for communication and sharing.

The risk of trying to force a child into an adult setting is that they will feel uncomfortable, may answer sparingly, and there is a long list of other biases that may jeopardize the purpose of your study (later in this book there's a chapter on bias (Chapter 2) and the chain of potential systematic distortions that can occur in a research setting). The opportunities and steps you can take are explained in the Chapter 3 on best practice.

Another book you can resort to for a more comprehensive introduction to research with children is *Researching Children's Experience: Methods and Methodological Issues* by psychology Professors Sheila Greene and Diane Hogan with the Trinity College Dublin, with contributions from Malcolm Hill and others (Sage 2005)[12].

---

[12]A section is available here: https://bit.ly/Greeneandhill

Also relevant in this context is *Designing for Children's Rights* – a global non-profit association, supporting the *Designing for Children's Rights Guide*,[13] which integrates children's rights into the design, business, and development of products and services around the world.

Furthermore, the Digital Futures Commission of the 5Rights Foundation in the UK has released a very comprehensive and helpful literature review by Senior Research Fellow at UCL Institute of Education Dr. Kate Cowan titled "A Panorama of Play" (2020) that supports the agenda to enable and nurture play for children in a digital world.[14]

Kids: a very picky and playful audience – and research target

Children's constant development makes for a moving research target.

The main topic of this book is how to include children (e.g., in product design and innovation) through research, regardless of the type of product or design or content as long as children are amongst the intended audience. That is easier said than done, and one of the challenges is in the very nature of childhood: as kids grow up, they constantly develop new skills and preferences and this challenges the including part, as research clearly needs to be tailored to the skills and abilities of the participants. Read more about the significance and insignificance of children's age as a descriptor in the section "Description bias" in Chapter 2.

One of the ways to move beyond age groups in general and specifically with a focus on research is to understand development deeper through the prism of play. The following section looks at different forms of play and ties this into research approaches.

A spectrum of play – and a spectrum for research

The LEGO Foundation[15] is a nonprofit organization that funds a wealth of research in play.

---

[13]The guide, nicknamed D4CR, is here: https://childrensdesignguide.org/

[14]Cowan, K. (2020). *A Panorama of Play – A Literature Review*. Digital Futures Commission. London: 5Rights Foundation. https://digitalfuturescommission.org.uk/wp-content/uploads/2020/10/A-Panorama-of-Play-A-Literature-Review.pdf

[15]The LEGO Foundation owns 25% of the shares in the LEGO Group and it owns and operates the LEGO House, an experience house in Billund that opened in September 2017 and is "designed to give LEGO fans of all ages the ultimate LEGO experience."

It has published a host of white papers about play and kids of all ages, for instance *Play facilitation: the science behind the art of engaging young children* by Jensen et al. (2019).[16]

The white paper offers several ways to understand play in the 3–6 years age range, and it informs us of ways in which research can make use of play.

Play – in the context of learning – can be understood as *free play*, *guided play*, *games*, and/or *instructed play*. To quote from the white paper:

> There are many ways to play, each with different roles for adults and children, and with each posing different demands on the players. The dynamic nature of play has led to some friction in the field. There are researchers who maintain free play as the "gold standard" and argue that adults' roles should be limited or non-existent. Others view guided play, in which adults hold a supportive role, also as play.

This distinction allows us to design our research depending on the nature of the behavior and feedback we wish to obtain from the kids. There are three types of research setup: free play, directed play, and guided play.

A free-play research setup

A free-play research setup has less structure and fewer instructions, and the adult researcher's role is to observe, listen to, and acknowledge children during play. The adult will intervene when children struggle, for example, to join peer play, explain their ideas or needs, make plans, or regulate their emotions. The kids set their own goals in the play, based on their interests. The setup allows them to be very active: explore, ask *what if*, reinvent ideas, and be creative.

As a researcher, you may start out by pointing to a specific play challenge or opportunity but not offer any approach or solution – you will leave it up to the kids to define the goal (likely implicitly through the play), the approach, and the outcome. This may require more time, space, and materials than more directed play approaches. You may also need to be extra diligent in matching kids with others with similar interests and abilities when the setup includes more than one child at a time.

---

[16]By Hanne Jensen, Angela Pyle, Jennifer M. Zosh, Hasina B. Ebrahim, Alejandra Zaragoza Scherman, Jyrki Reunamo, and Bridget K. Hamre www.legofoundation.com/media/1681/play-facilitation_the-science-behind-the-art-of-engaging-young-children.pdf

If we need to understand issues linked to executive functions, self-regulation, social skills, self-esteem, health and well-being, and how kids apply their spatial skills and mathematics, we lean toward a free-play research setup.

A directed-play research setup

In the directed-play setup, the adult initiates and directs, the child follows, so, overall, there is more structure and less choice. The adult researcher's role is to guide and scaffold the children's attempts, instruct, observe their efforts, and support them when they struggle to master the intended learning goal or skill.

This setup can be applied if we need to understand the degree to which kids master academic and socio-emotional skills, or if kids can achieve specific goals.

As a researcher, you can resort to conventional research tasks, for example, direct the child to do or find something, but be aware that this approach will only work well for as long as the child is engaged in the task.

A guided-play – or games – research setup

If we need to observe, build on, and extend children's thinking and ideas, the LEGO Foundation's white paper points to an approach that falls in between directed and free play, and which they refer to as guided play.

Guided play has an implicit learning focus – it has a goal, set by the adult, who is the one that creates the context and sets some boundaries around the play. This is why in some ways it resembles a game – it has a starting point (a state), some rules for moving forward, and sometimes also an agreed-upon endpoint (a different state). The roles are well defined; the children make the choosing (e.g., what to do and how) and the adult presents and interacts.

As a researcher, you can take your starting point in the children's own interests and support them in order to achieve one or more goals within a play context. The researcher needs to be mindful that the research questions, and their corresponding suggestions, must make sense in the play scenario.

Games

This approach may be more fun for children than the directed-play setup. Since the point of a game is to follow its specific rules, rather than the adult's rules, it can be experienced as more engaging if the children feel a higher level of autonomy. They may still, however, need adult assistance in understanding the rules.

As a researcher, you can choose this approach when you need to understand how children progress on a learning curve, from the early stages of grasping something new to gradually growing adept and dealing with more challenging tasks.

Choosing the right approach for any given research objective is one of the researcher's key considerations. To dive deeper into this topic, please refer to steps 4 and 5 in Chapter 2 on bias.

To find more inspiration on the topic of play, the National Literacy Trust, a charity organization in the UK, has issued several white papers on play and also a short overview: "10 reasons why play is important."[17]

Global research with children

As if it were already not complex enough for adult researchers to conduct research with children, carrying out the same research in cultures that are foreign to the researcher is even more complex. If you work on projects that require research from different markets or cultures around the globe, many questions and concerns will arise that are indeed foreign, ranging from the unfamiliar to the outlandish (pun intended). This section aims to highlight some of the main challenges and provide a starting point for tackling them in a practical way.

Truly global studies?

Few companies – if any – can afford (or are willing to invest the necessary time and money) to run truly global studies, if by global we mean including children who cover the entire spectrum of children's lives, not just *where* they live, but *how* they live. The first step in a structured global research approach is to determine the priorities – for example, if it is important to cover the major markets (a commercial priority and one that is likely rooted in figures that are at least a year old, if not more historical data) or to represent market diversity. If the first is the case, selecting the desired target geographies is clearly a very simple task (choose the top 3 or 5 or 10 grossing countries) but not necessarily the most sustainable approach, as one risks not opening one's eyes (and possibly one's innovation and market development) to the rest of the world, which will likely be bigger in both population and potential.

If it is a priority to reflect the diversity of the market in one's research, the following guidelines can help reduce the complexity of such an endeavour. The link of 18 bias areas presented in Chapter 2 can also serve as a reminder of the many decisions that are part of a research project and how and when cultural diversity can be a concern.

---

[17]https://literacytrust.org.uk/resources/10-reasons-why-play-important/

How children live

The challenge of being sensitive to how children live can be broken down into questions such as

- To which extent does *national or regional culture* matter for the child's experience of the product or service?

- Does *ethnic or group culture?*

- Does *family culture?*

Whether *national or regional culture* matters for the child's experience of the product or service will depend on factors such as national or regional:

- Legislature: Are the laws governing children significantly different across the globe or at least across our coverage area?

- Are the norms for children's behavior consistent?

- Are the traditions? Are the values?

Does *family culture* matter for the child's experience of the product or service? Or do we expect that the product or service is uniformly adopted (e.g., bought and consumed) across every family around the world? How will the experience differ in different family structures?

The extent to which children in a given culture belong to traditional family structures may also matter. It may have no significance to the child's experience whether or not the family is a more traditional nuclear family[18] or it may be very significant. For instance, in some family structures the father or mother may have certain specific roles in the parenting process. In other family structures there may not be a mother or a father at all. In some cases there may be no parent present at all, for example, if the children are raised by other family members or by the authorities. The point is to have an open approach to concepts such as family and parents.

---

[18]For a further exploration on the analogy between different contemporary family structures and the atomic model see Rahul Sharma's classification of families here: www.ncbi. nlm.nih.gov/pmc/articles/PMC4649868/

Research with foreign kids means working with foreign adults

The first point to recognize is one that permeates this book – that research with kids goes through their responsible adults. A study with kids in a foreign culture also means contacting moderators and recruiters. This clearly precedes the actual research and will be a contributing factor in the success or failure of the research project; the level of correct interpretation of your research needs by the these different groups of foreign adults (parents, moderators, recruiters, maybe interpreters as well) will determine the success of the initial steps of the study. It goes without saying that it is crucial that they understand the purpose and procedures that your project needs, but there are many other ways that your study can go wrong, and in requesting foreign assistance you will need to communicate much more explicitly and precisely than you'd need to with familiar assistants.

For instance, the understanding of a given methodology can be very different from one culture to another. User research is a well-established field in some countries, but less so in others – some may, for instance, confound user research with market research. If, for example, you expect the foreign children to work mainly on their own (the free-play research setup mentioned earlier) you'll need to make sure that your foreign assistants know this. In fact, you may need to check well ahead of time how free play is interpreted and expressed in that foreign culture.

On the one hand, you'll need to listen to local advice on how to set up the local study and, on the other, you'll need to adhere to the best practices. Choosing and supervising your local assistants is key in this effort. It may literally mean to seek "the best of both worlds." It may not be accomplished in the first go – you can reduce your risk by running a pre-study to make sure that everyone is on the same page, and you may need to set plenty of time aside for preparations, local adaptations and building shared references. It may help the locals if you can show them a video that illustrates how you'd like the session to run. If the test script is complex and full of precise language, you can verify its translation to the local language by having it translated back to the original language (by a different translator).

Language and translation

Sharing the same language (or rather, the lack of a shared language) is an illustrative example of how research across cultures is subject to more uncertainty and potentially also bias than within-culture research. If I am interested in studying in areas where I don't speak the language, I will need a translator or interpreter, either simultaneously or after the fact. My role will be that of an observer (Figure 1-1).

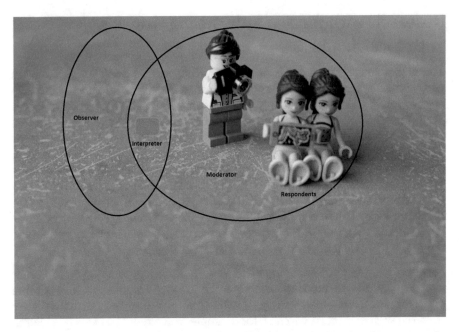

Figure 1-1. The quality of the interpretation will determine whether the observer gets the full story or only some parts of it (but which parts?), as a supplement to what the moderator can explain afterward or write in a report

Apart from being skilled and experienced in interpretation, the interpreter will need to have a firm grasp of the children's references, idioms, and vocabulary and must be able to translate that to the language we share. The extent to which the interpreter understands the children's references to their play universe, to their media, and to their situation in general is crucial. The deeper the translator's understanding, and the clearer this is communicated to observers, the better for the study. One way to increase the chances of having this higher level of understanding is to hire an interpreter who is a parent of children in the same age group as we study, or perhaps a bilingual teacher since they are trained to understand children and their ways of communicating. If faced with the hypothetical choice of either great technical translation (e.g., the syntax, grammar, vocabulary) or great child-world translation (e.g., the children's references and associations), one could argue that in some cases it is better to have the latter, since it may be the least accessible or most elusive. The point being that as an observer it is more important to understand what they mean than what they say. And also that good translation is more valuable than one might be aware of.

Culture has an impact on research with children in other and more subtle ways than spoken languages and shared references do.

Selecting which cultures to study

If you work on projects that need research from the main markets (or cultures) around the globe, you'll need a solid model for selecting which cultures to study. To some organizations, the model is simply to pick cultures based on market size or market value, for example, population or Gross Domestic Product (GDP, the total value of goods and services produced in a country), or the GDP per capita. This is certainly relevant from a business point of view, although the view is backward in time (how the markets were when the GDP was calculated, perhaps one or two years ago or even more) and does not necessarily take market trends and market potentials into account. Here I will suggest a different approach that is more sensitive to cultural differences than market sizes or values: an approach that recognizes that there are national and regional cultural groupings that affect the behavior of societies and organizations, and that these behaviors are persistent across time. I have found it helpful to keep this in mind when preparing research and discussing with project stakeholders where to go – and not go.

As a researcher, I have often come across two different lines of thought that have brought projects to simply go to the same cultures over and over again without really understanding or even considering why. One is that the team was culturally homogenous and it didn't occur to anyone that the results they could potentially get from going outside of that culture would be different and relevant. The other line of thought comes from stakeholders settling comfortably into one particular groove out of habit or in order to be able to directly compare new studies with previous ones and ignoring the bigger picture. For both of these cases a more structured and strategic approach to selecting where to go may not alter the outcome but it will help stakeholders to literally broaden their horizons and maybe discover new opportunities.

Selections based upon polarities

I often find it helpful in exploratory research (where differences and patterns in behavior or preferences are important) to consider polar opposites when it comes to the cultural perception of the underlying values of the product or service. In the example of a toy (or play proposition), where the value of play is important, I will look to cultures that are polar opposites when it comes to play in general (countries where play is either warmly encouraged and highly valued or the opposite) or to specific traits about the toy. If, for instance, it is designed for single play, I would consider researching the toy in cultures that prefer collectivistic play patterns.

The benefit from this approach is that the chances of finding meaningful differences and patterns is higher, since the duality or diversity is built into the study from the beginning. It assures that my stakeholders and I take a holistic approach and that we do not stay within our own culture.

If instead I relied on the approach of selecting based on market size, I would risk that my results are more uniform, perhaps even bland, which may be interesting if the purpose was to estimate the product's market appeal, but not in the context of innovation.

If it is hard to come up with polar opposites, there is help to be found from the Union of International Associations.[19] It sponsored an *Encyclopedia of World Problems and Potential*,[20] which includes a comprehensive list of issues relevant to the human kind (from anarchy, boredom, and creativity to xenophobia, youthfulness, and zealotry), and how those issues can be catalogued according to polar opposites. For example, one problem is the inadequate facilities for children's play,[21] which can be tied to a broad spectrum of factors (and ultimately how the different cultures value these differently): how schools and recreational areas (including parks, sports facilities, playgrounds, etc.) are funded and maintained, where they are located and how easy they are to get to, if they are scarce, free, clean, supervised, and so on.

Hierarchy

Different cultures have different perceptions of the hierarchy between parents and children. In my native culture, the hierarchical distance is shorter than in most other cultures, according to the power distance index of Gert Hofstede.[22] Children in Denmark (and other low power distance countries such as Sweden and New Zealand) will expect to be heard and included in decisions to a higher degree than in other high power distance cultures (such as Malaysia and Slovakia), and they will have a relatively higher disregard for formal hierarchy because that is the way they have been brought up. For instance, they will call their parents, teachers, and other adults by their first names, and they will not wait to speak until they have been spoken to. In high power distance cultures this behavior will be considered rude and the children disciplined. The significance to research of these differences is subtle but profound.

---

[19]The Union of International Associations (UIA, established in 1907) is a research institute and documentation center, founded by Henri la Fontaine (who received the Nobel Peace Prize in 1913) and Paul Otlet, a founding father of what is now called information science.

[20]http://encyclopedia.uia.org/en

[21]http://encyclopedia.uia.org/en/problem/138911

[22]Geert Hofstede (1928 -2020) was a Dutch social psychologist and professor who founded and managed the personnel research department of IBM Europe from 1965 to 1971. During which time he developed cultural dimensions based on a large international survey consisting of thousands of questionnaire responses from more than 60 countries addressing specific cultural issues. From the results, Hofstede developed a model whereby an individual country could be assigned a score on each of five dimensions, thus offering multiple ways of comparing various cultures. See also www.geert-hofstede.com and https://en.wikipedia.org/wiki/Geert_Hofstede

If I, in my low power distance culture, have planned a study in a high power distance culture, I need to revisit my expectations for the relationship between me (and potentially other members of my organization) and the researchers, moderators, translators, venue staff, and participants – adult accompaniment as well as child respondents. I cannot expect the same unbridled or open-hearted feedback or criticism from the high power distance children as from the children I am more used to. I may need to adapt the question guide or stimulus.

In a cross-cultural project, if we have different perceptions of the power distance, the way we communicate can be awkward or even diminished, and the research results will be skewed. To reduce this problem, all members of the research project, from client to recruiter, interpreter, evaluator, and moderator, need to have a clear understanding of possible obstacles related to power levels and how to organize around them.

It is important to communicate clearly to the accompanying adult which role they are expected to play. In the high power distance culture the parent may expect to – literally – speak on behalf of the child, so if this is not purposeful it needs to be addressed, for example, verbally or by the physical arrangement of the study (e.g., by placing the adult at a distance but within view from the child). Again, the need to communicate explicitly around this is even higher if the researcher originates from a culture at the opposite end of the power distance scale.

Point of reference

Another arena for potential misunderstandings in cross-cultural research is the point of reference, whether it is yourself (individualism) or your group (collectivism). This is a dimension that has been described in sociology (such as by Hofstede) as well as in psychology (for instance, by Richard E. Nisbett, an American social psychologist and writer[23]) and has significant implications for research with children.

For example, testing a toy in Denmark (highly individualistic) and in China (highly collectivistic) using the same research procedures can lead to problems. If, due to their general cultural characteristics, Danes speak mostly on their own behalf and Chinese speak mainly on the behalf of their group, the results might be incomparable.

---

[23]Nisbett's research interests range from social cognition, culture, and social class to aging. In *The Geography of Thought* (Free Press 2003), Nisbett builds on an analysis of ancient Greek and Chinese civilizations and how, for instance, it leads to differences in individualism/collectivism between Easterners and Westerners. See also https://en.wikipedia.org/wiki/Richard_E._Nisbett

To mitigate this issue in research design, I as a researcher from an individualist culture can encourage children to try to assess what would pose problems for others or for the society as a whole rather than to the respondent individually. Also, I could try to avoid concepts such as "problems" and "criticism" and instead focus on areas of improvements and increased harmony.

Gender or gender roles

Another example of potential misunderstanding is in the significance of gender and in the role of gender. In my native Danish culture, there is a general interest in minimizing the gap between the genders (what Hofstede calls a feminine culture, which can in itself be a misleading term). Bluntly put, we have a higher tolerance for manly women and womanly men than countries where the way a man or woman should dress, behave, smell, or work is more narrowly defined. The same applies to children and gender, and the tolerance for girly boys or boyish girls or nonbinary young people.

In a cross-cultural study, a misunderstanding can occur in the recruitment phase if, for instance, I, the Feminine-culture-researcher, will study children in a Masculine culture and I request from a local recruiter a 50-50 gender split of respondents, but the Masculine culture recruiter then insists that my topic is "a girls toy" and thus will supply only female respondents.

It's complex – but not impossible

Polarities can serve to make selection criteria more explicit and reduce the bias of selections based on prejudice or habit.

Considering polarities (e.g., classic dichotomies such as structured and flexible, responsible and free, supported and challenged) can also expand the themes or semantics of a study area in general, but certainly specifically to cross-cultural studies. It is important to be aware that factors like these are pervasive and exist on all levels – between the adults in a study, between the children, and between the adults and the children. In research with foreign children, you will experience a more complex research situation than if you were studying foreign adults. In fact, the complexity is twofold, resulting from both the cross-cultural and the adult–kid dimensions.

To sum up, if you work in an organization that operates in several cultures or if you need to run a study that has to include cultures in many markets, there are many practical and theoretical complexities that must be addressed. It requires the researcher to be sensitive to the smaller nuances, as well as to the larger, more obvious cultural differences, in every step of the research process, which we will go through in the next chapter.

How (Not) to Ruin Perfectly Good Research in 18 Steps

The greatest teacher, failure is.

—Yoda, *Star Wars: Episode VIII – The Last Jedi*[1]

Now we will dive head first into the key areas of potential bias – systematic distortion – in user research with children. I present them in the order that they would occur chronologically in a given project as a chain and then group

---

[1]True Star Wars fans will know that I am using the quote out of context. The context is Luke's dismissals of Rey's attempts to recruit him as a teacher and for him to rejoin the Resistance, and Yoda telling Luke to pass on what he has learned: "Strength, mastery, hmm… but weakness, folly, failure also. Yes: failure, most of all." (https://medium.com/@grelan/actual-quote-from-yoda-to-luke-in-the-last-jedi-regard-ben-solo-and-rey-that-resonated-with-me-db7945ad83c8)

© Thomas Visby Snitker 2021

T. V. Snitker, *User Research with Kids*, https://doi.org/10.1007/978-1-4842-7071-4_2

them into 18 steps. To be a master researcher one must understand and accept these biases and the failures they introduce in research with children.

When something suddenly happens around us, our fast mental processing makes us think and react as these processes, or biases, allow us to go quickly through cycles of reactions based upon how we receive, select, store, transform, develop, and recover information. By design (well, evolution) this process is constantly ongoing and can happen without us paying too much attention to it. Thus bias in some ways is a cognitive equivalent to what happens when your doctor tests your reflexes by pounding your knee, your leg is designed to jerk.

This chapter may unintentionally leave you with the thought that qualitative research is so prone to bias that one might just as well not engage in qualitative research altogether. However, one must not give up hope – even though there are hundreds of ways that research can fail, we can still prepare well and execute well and get it right most of the time.

Inclusivity and diversity – no-brainers in research

Inclusivity and diversity are no-brainers in research, but unfortunately not everywhere else.

There are sometimes legitimate reasons for research to be exclusive and nondiverse, or for it to remain within the researcher's or stakeholders' own circles, whether regarding social issues, gender, abilities, ethnicity, or other. Overcoming these obstacles does require extra effort and may also necessitate higher costs, extra time, interpretation, and more specific moderating skills.

These constraints are universal and are ingrained in qualitative researchers. I expect all researchers to be fully aware of the biases that a small-scale study introduces and to be able to explain these to their stakeholders. I hope that many researchers also feel equipped to challenge those stakeholders who constantly remain within their own circles, which can then come to serve as echo chambers, and that as a part of the scoping phase the researcher will educate the stakeholders of the pros and cons of less vs. more inclusive studies.

Simply put, limited or short-sighted research has reduced effectiveness and relevance as it does not reflect on the wider audiences and only points to a portion of the whole. If you are in the market to buy a car, you wouldn't choose one that only drives on paved roads. If you are designing a TV commercial, you wouldn't settle for one that only displayed on the latest TV sets. The challenge when commissioning research is to maintain an inclusive mindset regardless of the budget and time constraints.

So what are some ways you can inspire skeptical or frugal stakeholders to be more inclusive?

- If the brief from the stakeholder overlooks inclusivity, simply add to the scope the elements that you feel are missing. This will force the stakeholder to actively consider if they really wish to discard inclusivity.

- Frame inclusivity as innovation. Since looking in new directions can lead to new ideas, inclusivity can boost innovation, and that makes sense on a business level.

- Build a business case that demonstrates the costs of the lost opportunity, for example, that the research, once it is scaled up, can identify all business-relevant audiences and needs. For instance, if the world market for a given product is €100 million, but on the small-scale budget you're only able to include 40% of the market, the stakeholder is essentially risking and gambling with €60 million. Is the stakeholder willing to do this?

- Frame inclusivity as future-proofing. As societies develop, so do fringe segments – and they may even grow into a key segment in the future.

- Inclusivity and diversity are "hot topics" in most developed markets. Not recognizing this means being out of touch with current trends.

- Use the bias chain (see the next section) to map out the strengths and weaknesses of your research portfolio – are there any signs of systematic distortion? Can you mitigate these risks?

The bias chain: Is bias a feature or a bug?

No one can ever honestly claim to run completely bias-free qualitative research. Conversely, such a claim to me seems like an open invitation to scrutiny – now I am really curious to find "the holes in the cheese" and eager to roast the study's findings in the flames of perpetual argument. Even if I agree with those findings, the end doesn't justify the means when it comes to research. Instead, researchers must start by addressing the devil they don't know, and keep on doing so throughout the process. Better the devil you know than the devil you don't.

Bias is the unfair preference for, or prejudice against, one person or group; it is a systematic distortion. It would be unfair to your stakeholders if you – whether you realize it or not – gave recommendations on a shaky or even faulty foundation.[2] It would be unfair to your respondents not to offer them the best possible ways to give their feedback. It would be unfair to yourself not to make your best effort. A poor study could even reflect badly on all your fellow researchers within and outside of your community. But despair not: you can address those fleeting, evading, elusive biases that are hard to notice by going through your process from start to finish with a laser-sharp focus on the potential problems. Here's a framework to get you started. It begins with the scoping phase and continues through preparations, execution, reporting, and beyond.

Bias in the scoping phase

Steps in this phase

> 1 For the right stakeholders or client
>
> 2 The right objective or problem or pain or goal
>
> 3 The right product or project

1 For the right stakeholders or client

This is where the bias chain starts. It is a weak link if the client or stakeholders strongly oppose the main features of the study (e.g., the scope, approach, process, and method), making it likely that the client at some point will reject the study altogether. Fortunately, this is rare, but it does happen. And if you experience it, you will find it is a very good time to reevaluate the feasibility of your study, and perhaps abandon it altogether if necessary.

The right stakeholder or client is a person or group that will treat the findings with the right level of confidentiality, will trust the process and will trust the researchers – someone with a commitment to see the research through.

2 The right objective or problem or pain or goal

The right objective to seek, or problem to solve, is one with business impact, one that is realistic and can be studied in a timely and economically sound manner. Most companies have plenty of pains, but not all of them can be solved by mere research. As a researcher, I often find myself guiding stakeholders on how to establish the most rewarding cost/benefit ratio between the study and its potential outcome – and this sometimes leads to the end of the research project. Also, I often wonder if I am serving the

---

[2]For the etymology of bias: www.etymonline.com/word/bias

stakeholders' needs or if I'm serving their wants, or if, in fact, their wants and needs are actually the same – if they actually need a different approach or scope than what they request. It will be better for all parties involved if this is straightened out as soon as possible.

Not all pains or problems are created equal: what is right for one stakeholder is not necessarily right for another. What at one point seems like a problem may not be so at a later point. At the very outset of any research project, the researcher and stakeholders must agree on a robust description of the objective – to do otherwise is to risk producing research that serves no one and solves no problems at all. It may well be that the research was otherwise successful, but if nobody cared about the outcome, the results will ultimately be futile.

See also Step 5: "The consensus bias"

3 The right product or project

This link in the chain simply deals with selecting which product or project to research. Getting this right may sound easy, but it can be tricky. Deciding what to include and exclude is of course of fundamental importance in a research project.

Selection bias

You'll probably be asking yourself or the stakeholders various questions, such as: Is it the entire product life cycle – the entire user experience? Is it just the first time experience? Does it include documentation such as manuals or web pages? Should we test it against a benchmark, such as a competing product? Who decides in this selection (acceptance or rejection, scoping it smaller or larger) – and on what grounds?

Often, due to time or budget restraints or practicalities, you will find that you are only able to cover parts of the relevant product in your study, and in that case it is essential to have a very clear definition of, and justifications for, what to leave in or out of the study. This selection and rejection in itself introduces bias and likely happens when you are at maximum capacity (which you probably are most of the time for business reasons, oh and also according to Parkinson's law: "Work expands to fill the time available for its completion"[3]).

So if you need to choose, which project will it be? The one that can provide the most impact? The one that can influence the most stakeholders? The one that has you working on the firmest ground (familiar methodology, familiar

---

[3]https://en.wikipedia.org/wiki/Parkinson%27s_law – make sure to read the other hilarious corollaries

target audience, familiar research setup, etc.)? Or the one that has the most return on investment (if you have any way of assessing this in any realistic way)? All of these reasons are valid in themselves, so it is not an easy choice; being aware of your selection biases will help you make a better decision.

Bias during the preparation phase

Steps in this phase:

4 The right respondents, described in the right terms

5 Doing the right things

6 ...at the right time of day or week or month

7 ...for the right duration

8 ...in the right location/setting

9 ...using the right device

4 The right participants, described in the right terms

The researcher (often together with the stakeholders) makes numerous and important decisions when deciding how to describe the respondents. How to define who will be included and who will be left out of the research project? Poor screening and recruiting procedures create biased samples, while random sampling during recruiting reduces sample bias. And as a general rule, being aware of bias is key when screening in respondents you want and screening out those who don't fit.

Sampling bias

In qualitative research, we often use a word borrowed from quantitative research when selecting who to invite as respondents, a sample. A sample in quantitative research refers to a smaller, manageable version of a larger group: it is a subset containing the characteristics of a larger population. A biased sample consists of respondents who do not represent the group of interest (or at least not to an adequate extent). In other words, you are studying the wrong people.

The word sample, however, can be somewhat deceptive. It is really more appropriate when used in the term blood sample. In this case, a sample of blood from an individual is similar to all the blood in that person's body (we expect it to be similar). In qualitative research, on the other hand, if we ask for opinions from, or study the behavior of, one individual in a given society, we will not expect the opinions or behavior to be very similar to all of the other members of that society. So the word sample can be misleading, and you should always make sure that you and your stakeholders agree on your approach. (See also the section "Descriptions inherited from market research.")

The two main things to keep an eye on in the recruitment process are (1) the pool, list, or population from which people are drawn (consider how it has been created and what bias that creation – or the formulation of the creation – might have introduced), and (2) how we select from that pool (and what bias that selection introduces).

The most common sampling methods we use in qualitative research are all more or less prone to bias. Let's have a look at each in more detail.

Come over for tea!

Convenience Sampling: Respondents are selected based on availability or other factors that appeal to the researcher (Figure 2-1). For example, as a student you might recruit fellow students, simply because they are at hand. In kids research, you might ask your personal friends and family if they know kids who can participate.

Figure 2-1. There are always some respondents who are easier to access than others, at least from the point of view of the researcher (who evidently has easy access to rows and rows of hairless plastic people!)

The researcher may be implicitly or explicitly biased in favor of, or against, specific personalities. Practicalities may determine that only people in the researcher's vicinity are selected. The practicalities associated with the study may systematically skew the selection toward certain groups, for example, people who are able to participate during regular working hours, or people that the researcher has some kind of a relationship with. This is clearly not geared toward producing results that can be generalized. But the approach has the advantage of being the lowest common denominator of all sampling, a convenient starting point without any barriers for the researcher.

Volunteers wanted!

If you post a request for volunteers and obtain voluntary responders, you have saved a lot of time and energy in finding respondents (Figure 2-2).

Figure 2-2. The researcher has asked for volunteers among the hairless plastic people. (The study is apparently very popular.)

The bias in this approach has less to do with the researcher's personal network (compared to Convenience sampling) and more to do with the volunteers. Could there be implicit or explicit reasons for some groups of people to volunteer and other groups not to? Perhaps extraverts are more likely to come forward than introverts. Perhaps people who have prior experience with the domain or product at hand are more likely than people who do not.

Or perhaps people who have no other plans are more likely to volunteer than "busy" people.

Help me find the next respondent!

Snowball Sampling, or Chain Referral: the researcher chooses the first respondent (following one of the two methods above) who then finds and recruits the next respondent, and so on (Figure 2-3).

Figure 2-3. One hairless plastic respondent recruits the next and so on

This allows the researcher to get to audiences that can be hard to find using regular methods. Also, it is usually cheaper but often requires more time, as you are reliant on other people taking time out to help you.

The bias here is similar: there are implicit or explicit reasons for some groups of people to volunteer and other groups not to.

I want you in my study!

Purposive Sampling, or Judgment Sampling, is when the researcher uses their personal judgment in including or excluding potential respondents in a qualitative study, often in order to cover a range of different perspectives, for example, to hear the most diverse voices possible regardless of how niche they may be, or actually, actively seeking out niche voices (Figure 2-4).

Figure 2-4. Purposive sampling

Derek Zinger, who helped tremendously in the review of this book, remarks that it's good to know that even among hairless plastic people we can still find unique individuals!

Other sampling concepts

Here are some other relevant concepts that you may come across in market research, opinion polls, or similar, where your results need to reflect the entire population, but which are less relevant in the context of user research. They are mentioned here only in passing in the hope that you can advise your stakeholders not to use these concepts in the wrong context – hence no hairless plastic people illustrations.

Random sampling

The researcher chooses using random selection from all individuals in a population, like "drawing lots." Every respondent has the same chance of being selected.

This method obviously only works insofar as the researcher actually has access to data or responses from all the individuals, which is rare if the population is large (e.g., adult males between 20 and 55 years of age) or dispersed (e.g., everyone who has not tried a given product before). The randomness of the selection aims to reduce the bias, and truly random sampling is therefore a desirable attribute in quantitative studies that aim to make valid statistical inferences about an entire population.

Stratified sample

The researcher chooses from a specific list of random people.

This sampling method is appropriate when the population has mixed characteristics, and you need to ensure that every characteristic (e.g., gender, age range) is proportionally represented in the sample.

From the overall proportions of the population, you calculate how many people should be sampled from each subgroup. Then you select a sample from each subgroup.

This process (widely applied in opinion polls and political surveys) is meaningful in research with children in those cases where the study must precisely reflect the diversity of the population of children, for example, based on their ages, preferences, or skills. Rather than taking a random sample from all the kids, the aim is first to sort them into various subgroups, and then, in the selection process, to be very specific (but subjective) in picking from all the subgroups.

The result is much less bias, but it comes at a much higher effort (in time and in cost) than with the four main approaches.

There is a pitfall to this approach, however. In qualitative research, we often study psychological qualities such as how people understand a message or product, how they derive meaning from it and which values they attribute to it. We often want to understand if people react differently to the same product or message, and why. We wish to analyze their interpretations. In these cases, in these research domains, we are more interested in people's personalities and their past experiences (e.g., if they have tried something similar before and if they have some sort of training), and at the same time, we are very careful about how much we inform and prime them ahead of time. It can be very tricky to ask people if they are aware of a certain phenomenon (a strata) without... well, making them aware of it!

Description bias

Sampling is also prone to bias as the very description of a given target audience depends upon how well the researcher and stakeholder understand this audience ahead of time; this understanding may be flawed, prejudiced, or skewed.

Note that there's a fine line between bias (the systematic distortion) and "implicity," which refers to the quality or state of being implicit or implied, rather than directly or explicitly stated.

Bias changes over time as societies change. A generation ago a popular riddle went like this:

A father and son are in a horrible car crash that kills the dad. The son is injured and rushed to the hospital. Just as he's about to go under the knife, the surgeon says, "I can't operate – that boy is my son!"

As time passed and more women became doctors and same-sex marriages became more usual, the point of the riddle declined, but even today a doctor in many people's minds is a man. This was demonstrated as recent as 2014 in a study published by Boston University.[4] There were (and apparently still are) doctors and female doctors. It is likely the same with nurses and male nurses, the national handball team and the national women's handball team. This bias is not only old-fashioned, but also – from the point of view of this book – a potential practical (and, as I will soon argue, cognitive) problem. If your stakeholders specify doctors, nurses, or national handball team players as the target audience, do they then imply gender or not?

To be very detailed about description bias, let's use the term doctor as an example of bias and implicity. Imagine a study that needs "doctors"; a closer look at the description "doctor" reveals an ambiguity in other ways beyond gender:

Any given doctor will always be a doctor, because it is a title given to a person who graduated with a medical degree, but the description does not say if the study needs someone who works as a doctor, or only works part-time, or serves as a volunteer doctor, or has retired as a doctor. Who's to say which of these qualify as a doctor and which do not? We might argue that the full-time working doctor was implicit – something that should have been made explicit in order to reduce ambiguity (as *doctor* can also describe nonworking doctors). But the bias is more subtle and is something that the stakeholders in the study may not have been aware of at all: they themselves are working, so they are naturally thinking of other people who are working. Ergo, the doctor they need is working.

You may find the example trivial and specific to... well, studies with doctors. But there's something much larger at stake which is playing tricks with our minds: metaphors, figures of speech,[5] tropes, and allegories. (See also the section "Metaphorically speaking"). In the 1980s, American psychologists and

---

[4]www.bu.edu/articles/2014/bu-research-riddle-reveals-the-depth-of-gender-bias/
[5]A "figure of speech" is of course a metaphor in itself, except on the rare occasions where one speaks while blowing bubblegum bubbles – thus creating actual speech figures (well, speech *spheres*). Here's how-to in case you forgot: www.wikihow.com/Blow-a-Bubble-with-Bubblegum

linguists such as George Lakoff[6] founded the field of cognitive linguistics, and in books such as *Metaphors We Live By* (University of Chicago Press 2008) he and coauthor Mark Johnson examine metaphors.

They argue that metaphors "... are a fundamental mechanism of mind that allows us to use what we know about our physical and social experience to provide understanding of countless other subjects. Because such metaphors structure our most basic understandings of our experience, they are 'metaphors we live by' – metaphors that can shape our perceptions and actions without our ever noticing them."[7]

Which is why the doctor riddle used to work in the past: a doctor was always male, the profession worked as a metaphor for a specific gender, and we knew this from one personal experience after another. It wasn't that the laws of physics or society explicitly prohibited female doctors, but rather the general consensus based on experience was simply (and obviously wrongly) that "doctors" only came in one gender. And so we have come full circle – you can't take the "meta" out of the metaphor.

But once people and society changed, the metaphorical aspect lost its meaning. The other aspect of the doctor as someone working (actively practicing medicine), however, is still present.

The point is that when we describe our audience, and thus our respondents (doctors, nurses, or otherwise), we must look very carefully at the words we use in our descriptions. Let's now look at another example closer to the theme of this book; now you need to find children for a study. The level of ambiguity and abstraction is equally high as for the doctor example, yet I will argue that many studies with kids use this crude definition, often with gender and/or age group added.

But age is a very fickle parameter. A child who is one day younger than seven years old is roughly 15% older than a child who just turned six. The yearly changes within a group of kids that are "the same age" obviously increase the younger they are. Contrary to, for instance, people in their 50s, who, from age 50 to 59 also grow roughly 15% older (but in ten years instead of one).

Age, development, and the way that societies raise their children can also have profound effects, and we are not always aware of them.

One is the relative age effect. In one of his many noteworthy books, *Outliers: The Story of Success* (Back Bay Books 2008), the writer Malcolm Gladwell describes how significant just a few months in birthdate is in athletics and

---

[6]You are reading a footnote about George Lakoff. I am very happy to see that. You may enjoy his page on Wikipedia – it is here: https://en.wikipedia.org/wiki/George_Lakoff
[7]The quote is from the book's page on Amazon: www.amazon.com/Metaphors-We-Live-By-ebook/dp/B009KA3Y6I/

other domains such as academia and politics. When kids are very young and – in one example – start playing ice hockey, the kids are placed in age groups either based on the calendar year or academic year of their birth. Those born in the first quarter are generally marginally more developed than those born later. The small advantages of the first-quarter kids are recognized by coaches and they are given more attention and feedback than the slightly younger kids, and as this training and grooming goes on over the years, it generally allows the first-quarter kids to advance further. This explains why most top athletes are born in the first two quarters of a year in countries where the intake period follows the calendar and the last two quarters in countries where the intake follows the academic calendar from August to July.

This is not to say that age is a meaningless way to describe kids and differentiate between kids in research, but rather that it comes with limitations and with potential bias.

Descriptions inherited from market research

Finding the right respondents for a qualitative study most often requires some level of translation between the abstract definition suitable for describing the group (e.g., kids who are into animals) and the description of an individual who belongs to that group (one kid who is into animals). The individual will have general traits in common with the group, but at the same time the individual will also have traits that are more specific and subjective than the group's. For example, the animal-loving child may mainly be into cats, and in particular cats that are cute, but the group per definition has a much broader focus.

Selecting one single individual as an exemplar or representative of the group has larger effects in qualitative research, where the count of respondents is usually fairly small (e.g., 5, 10, or 20), than in quantitative research, which tends to count respondents in the hundreds and thousands, and in effect diluting the characteristics of the individual response in the overall result. It can thus lead to problems in the recruitment process for a qualitative study, if the respondent descriptions are inherited from a market perspective. This is likely to happen in companies and organizations that are marketing driven.

As a qualitative researcher you will likely also see it when working together with a marketing department – you will perhaps notice that the language is not about "users" and "experiences" but "audience" and "messages." Market research is interested in consumer behavior and aims to identify their needs[8] and uncover demographic, economic, and statistical information about a

---

[8]Here is one good source for a comparison of market research and user research: https://medium.com/reassemble/market-research-vs-user-research-are-they-the-same-3ec59dec637f.

specific industry, and must thus concern itself with a broad population of many individuals. User research, in contrast, aims to understand how someone does what task, why, and with what outcome. The problem is that there are many commonalities in the descriptions of the respondents in both approaches, but also many pitfalls, if you try to translate directly from one to the other.

Skill level as a descriptor

Skill level as a recruitment criterion is a rich source of bias. As an example, let's take computer skills. As the previously mentioned Jakob Nielsen describes in a review of a 2016 OECD report on computer skills in different countries,[9] you, dear reader, likely are very skillful, perhaps even an expert computer user. You know how to delete an email, for example, whereas 14% of the OECD audience in the study didn't. This is just one example of how using your own skills as a yardstick or reference point in a qualitative study can introduce significant bias into user experience research.

One way to overcome this hurdle is to describe the different segments of your audience according to their own skills.

The Dreyfus Model of Skill Acquisition[10] (later adapted in many ways, e.g., the Novice to Expert Theory), first proposed by brothers Hubert and Stuart Dreyfus (in 1980[11] and refined in *Mind over Machine*, Free Press, 1988), says that a student passes through the following five distinct stages:

1. Novice: You have to rely on rules, and your understanding of your own situation as well as your ability to exercise judgment is limited.

2. Advanced beginner: You begin to have some situational understanding but still struggle to prioritize different areas.

3. Competent: You accumulate information better, and you are able to consider a holistic view to make plans and to perform multiple tasks.

---

[9]www.nngroup.com/articles/computer-skill-levels/
[10]https://en.wikipedia.org/wiki/Dreyfus_model_of_skill_acquisition
[11]Since the work of the Dreyfus brothers was supported by the US Air Force, it needed to be unclassified in order to be made public. The original machine-typed documents with added approval stamps and signatures has been scanned and is available here: https://apps.dtic.mil/dtic/tr/fulltext/u2/a084551.pdf – worth a look for its authenticity alone.

4. Proficient: Your decision-making happens at a more intuitive than analytical level, therefore faster and requiring less effort.

5. Expert: You have an ingrained understanding of the situation, of its limitations and possibilities, and of what you need to do.

Throughout the learning stages there are four binary qualities, so-called mental functions, that help determine the skill level. As the Dreyfuses state:

Each of the four mental functions has a primitive and a sophisticated form and the functions are so ordered that attaining the sophisticated form of each presupposes the prior attainment of the sophisticated form of all those lower numbered in the ordering.[12]

I will try to illuminate them with examples from learning to ride a bicycle:

- Recollection (nonsituational or situational)

  As a novice you'll try to adhere to the main rules: tread the pedals and steer at the same time. As an advanced beginner you'll know to point the bicycle in a favorable direction (e.g., away from a curb or obstacle) before you tread and steer.

- Recognition (decomposed or holistic)

  The advanced beginner will struggle to match the speed and the balance of the bike with the steering and the direction, and will feel overwhelmed at times.

- Decision (analytical or intuitive)

  The competent bike rider will still need to analyze a situation carefully before making decisions, especially if new factors in traffic, surface, or weather emerge. The time and mental energy it takes to analyze the situation will limit the speed and confidence of the rider if you compare to the proficient or expert bike rider, who in contrast will ride more intuitively, "without the need for conscious calculation."

- Awareness (monitoring or absorbed)

---

[12]A Five-Stage Model of the Mental Activities Involved in Directed Skill Acquisition

The proficient bike rider will still need to monitor the situation and the surroundings whereas the expert rider will not. The Dreyfuses say that the analytical mind, relieved of its monitoring role in producing and evaluating performance, is quieted so that the performer can become completely absorbed in their performance. To me it echoes that feeling of flow – of "being on autopilot" in a good way, where you have been doing something for a while at a completely capable level but fully occupied with other things. A good source on flow is *Flow: The Psychology of Optimal Experience* (1997) by Hungarian-American psychologist Mihaly Csikszentmihalyi. It establishes *flow* as a state where the levels of challenge and skills are high and it introduces the beautiful model shown in Figure 2-5.

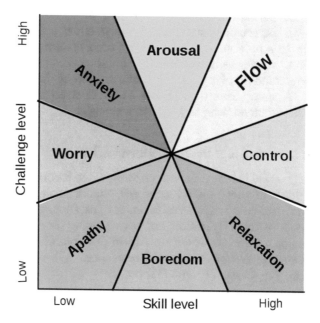

Figure 2-5. Notice flow in the top right area: a state where the levels of challenge and skills are both high. Source: `https://commons.wikimedia.org/wiki/File:Challenge_vs_skill.svg`

Combined in a table, the Dreyfus model looks like this:

| Skill level

Mental function	Novice	Advanced beginner	Competent	Proficient	Expert
Recollection	Nonsituational	Situational	Situational	Situational	Situational
Recognition	Decomposed	Decomposed	Holistic	Holistic	Holistic
Decision	Analytical	Analytical	Analytical	Intuitive	Intuitive
Awareness	Monitoring	Monitoring	Monitoring	Monitoring	Absorbed

This approach is useful when selecting and describing your respondent groups in the way it covers everyone in the target audience – everyone is a new beginner at some point, and through steady usage of, or exposure to, the product, they "graduate" to competent, proficient, and, later – through repeated use of perhaps not just one brand or make but also of the competition – to expert or super user. The term super user originates in IT, where it refers to a person who is an expert on a system. Here, however, I use the term in a broader sense to describe someone with an extensive (if not complete) understanding of a given product (or even of the marketplace for that product). A super user thus serves as an illustrative contrast to the novice, the inexperienced user, or users-in-training.

Service skills are not the same as platform skills

This is especially useful in research with children when it comes to researching digital experiences, as these experiences will require some level of skill and mastery of the particular digital platform, for instance, a gaming console (Xbox, Nintendo Switch, PlayStation, etc.) or a gaming service portal (Steam, Apple Arcade, etc.), a social network platform (TikTok, LEGO Life, etc.), or plainly the operating system of smartphones (e.g., iOS and Android) and computers (iOS, Windows, Chrome OS, etc.).

If setting out to test an experience on one of these platforms, it is important to understand how children with little or no experience with the platform will experience the service as this – the initial experience – will be the experience of every new child on the service in the future. It is equally important to understand the experience of children with some past platform experience and that of those children who have used the platform many times. This widespread distribution of skill levels makes it necessary to have a robust methodology to establish precisely which type of platform experience one is studying.

This leaves two types of skill levels (domains) for consideration when recruiting respondents (Figure 2-6):

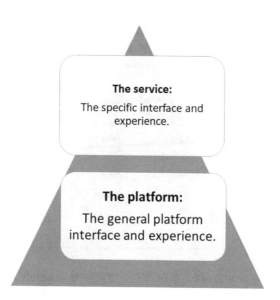

Figure 2-6. Two types of skill levels

1. Platform skills: For example, to which extent have the children played other games on this platform before?

2. Service skills: For example, to which extent have the children played this specific game before?

In my example before, where one is testing the service, it is easy to be overly focused on the service skills and neglectful of the platform skills when describing the respondents. I have used a pyramid as a metaphor for this issue since the service sits on the platform and since this fact might highlight the relationship between the two domains and the fact that children will acquire (general) platform skills *before* they acquire (specific) service skills. The point is, simply, as a researcher in charge of testing the service (as opposed to testing the platform), one should be mindful not to look for respondents solely with an eye for their service-related skills.

Skill distribution patterns

If you work in a well-established area (e.g., a content domain or technology that is more than 10 years old and is highly mature, such as, for instance, TV, washing machines, or theater) you will expect few novices (although newbies will likely come in on a regular basis) and many super users. And vice versa if you work in innovation: perhaps there are no super users of the brand new technology at all (yet), and almost everyone is a novice (at least for while).

Here are some very generalized estimates on audience skill distribution from my home country of Denmark to get you started thinking about how skills may be distributed among your audience:

	Novice	Advanced beginner	Competent	Proficient	Expert
TV sets	None	Few	Few	Most	Many
Pianos	Most	Few	Few	Few	Few
Door handles[13]	Few (none?)	Few	Few	Most	Many
Computers	Some	Some	Some	Few	Few
Some new technology	Most	Few	Few	Few	Few (none?)

When considering which are the possible domains of children being Proficient or Expert users, the area of learning in itself comes to mind. The sheer amount of areas that require them to learn – through rules or trial and error – on a daily basis is overwhelming to an adult. A given 6-year-old child needs to learn spoken language (maybe several languages), written language, traffic, shoe laces, tooth brushing, table manners, numbers, maybe a sport or several, sociality and relationship plus all the topics at school, and many other topics.

The term "digital natives," coined by Mark Prensky[14] in 2001, is used to describe the generation of people who grew up in the era of ubiquitous technology, including computers and the Internet, and it points to areas where contemporary children have an advantage compared to earlier generations. However, it is important that this term does not fool us – today's children are by no means digital proficients or digital experts, although many 6-year-old children spend more time with iPads than with, say, toothbrushes and shoe laces.

Another domain in which children – and especially preschoolers – excel is imagination and pretense. Their superpowers allow many kids to travel far and wide without moving and to assume all kinds of identities and traits at lightspeed. Similar to learning, imagination is a skill that requires nurturing and practice, and the support from the surrounding adults and playmates, so they are not equally distributed among the child population. These skills are important to remember when describing the type of respondents your project needs. Perhaps your product favors children that skew toward the more

---

[13]This makes for a splendid occasion to point to Don Norman and his book *The Design of Everyday Things* (BasicBooks, 1988) – a must read, also for its section on the design of door handles.
[14]https://en.wikipedia.org/wiki/Marc_Prensky

learning type or toward the more imaginative type – or toward both types. If there are main aspects of learning or imagination in the experience you will be testing, it may be necessary to be explicit about these aspects when recruiting children to your study.

To some extent the audience groups itself according to the technology adoption life cycle model (Figure 2-7),[15] from innovators to early adopters to (early and late) majority and laggards (a term that feels a little antiquated today), often depicted as a bell curve (see illustration). The model has an interesting background in that it was originally developed by agricultural researchers in the 1950s in the Study of the Diffusion of Farm Practices.[16] It was later published as the Diffusion of Innovation (DOI) Theory, developed by E.M. Rogers in 1962.[17,18]

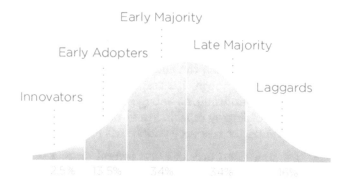

Figure 2-7. The innovation adoption life cycle

---

[15]Illustration Source: CC BY 2.5, `https://en.wikipedia.org/w/index.php?curid=11484459`

[16]The report summarized the categories as

innovators – had larger farms, were more educated, more prosperous, and more risk-oriented

early adopters – younger, more educated, tended to be community leaders, less prosperous

early majority – more conservative but open to new ideas, active in community, and influence to neighbors

late majority – older, less educated, fairly conservative, and less socially active

laggards – very conservative, had small farms and capital, oldest and least educated

[17]`https://en.wikipedia.org/wiki/Diffusion_of_innovations`

[18]There's also a more detailed account here: `https://livinghistoryfarm.org/farminginthe50s/crops_02.html`

The fact that the domain, product group or technology is well established obviously doesn't mean that this distribution with few novices and many super users is all encompassing and society wide. Mature technologies such as fighter jets, MR scanners, and nuclear power plants will likely also have few novices and many super users, but that is simply because the audience or user group is so small, while the requirement for training is so large, and also because operating the systems is an occupation. In addition, the users of these systems are likely more interested in simply using the systems as prescribed in the manual, rather than having an experience – the experience scores for training-intense areas such as fighter jets and nuclear power plants should document whether manuals are adhered to and if the staff is doing what they trained to do, or not.

Skill or *frequency of task*

Another recruitment approach I have found useful in user research (and not in market research) is using a description of respondents' frequency of task, which simply refers to how often the audience performs the given task. For instance, is a task frequent enough that respondents clearly remember what they did last time? Is it even frequent enough to consider them super users (someone who is extraordinarily capable in a given system and who is viewed by other people as a superior resource within that realm)?

If you have performed a given task daily or several times a week, and have done so for some time, the level of understanding and the skills you have accumulated allow you to have a clearer set of expectations and a large frame of reference. It may have improved your vocabulary in this area. It may have exposed you to several similar systems in which those tasks are performed. This knowledge and these skills can make you an excellent respondent – one who has all the resources for providing a lot of relevant feedback in depth as well as in breadth, and in exploratory research these resource-rich respondents can be extremely valuable. So, although this group may not matter much in the overall user population (e.g., because the resource-rich users are a small niche) it may very well be a priority to include them in the study. Also, it may be the case that the rest of the population will become resource-rich over time, and thus the insights you will have from the resource-rich are no longer niche. So even if from a market size perspective the resource-rich may not be an attractive research target, they may still be very relevant from a research perspective given the potential insights they can provide.

Staticity bias

It is often surprisingly hard to pigeonhole people when we all live such dynamic lives. Even seemingly static descriptions, such as a "doctor" or "car owner," can change overnight, or may be too open for interpretation and require a surprisingly detailed description of inclusion and exclusion criteria.

The descriptions of audiences can introduce bias, for instance, when they are too narrow or too static. If the description stipulates that an individual can only be in one subgroup at a time, then there will be bias toward research domains that are static, as opposed to domains where people frequently change their status dynamically. For instance, if you are testing a snack you may describe your audience as "hungry people," but their condition will change from being "famished" to "a little peckish" to "full" over the course of very little time. These attributes may be dynamic, but they are very real. In contrast, the description of the audience for the snack may be stated simply as "people who eat snacks at some interval." They either do or do not, and so we are ultimately talking about a very static attribute. Who's to say what would happen in a research study with non-snackers that took place well after regular meals and with snacks in front of them?

Staticity is especially significant when it comes to research with kids, as they by definition are in the middle of the dynamic development of growing up. What they liked or cared about yesterday may not be what they like today or tomorrow. But then again it may be, so it's best to be extremely precise when you describe which audience you wish to recruit for your study.

Respondents in research are similar to the raw materials, or main ingredients, in cooking, and how they are described and selected will tremendously influence the outcome. The preconceptions of the researcher and stakeholder may bias how this qualification or disqualification of respondents happens.

Additionally, bias can be introduced into the audience descriptions simply due to the fact that they are defined by the researcher, as opposed to being formulated by the respondents themselves. For example, the researcher is looking for doctors or people who own a car – not people who think they're doctors or who imagine they know what it's like to own a car. If they are a recently retired doctor or just sold their car yesterday, should they be included or excluded from the study? But if the researcher has limited knowledge of what it means to be (or think like or feel like) a doctor or relies on faulty, overly rigid, or loose definitions of what constitutes a doctor, a car owner, or a snacker, the sampling will clearly be biased.

The bias of gatekeepers and professional respondents

Professional respondents also cause sample bias. As adults, they typically show up in consumer studies such as focus groups. Their goal is to earn a part-time salary from the focus group and survey incentives, and they are biased in the way that they approach the study. They will try to adapt their opinions or behavior to fit in and to comply with what they expect you want.

In kids research, there's also the fact to consider that you are recruiting the kids through someone else, often a parent or teacher, and that person may have interests similar to those of being a professional respondent, or simply other interests that differ from those of the actual participating child. Also, the gatekeeping adult may simply be out of touch with the child's current preferences and hence unable to give accurate information during the screening process.

You can reduce the bias of the gatekeeper and when recruiting professional respondents in several ways:

- When you screen potential respondents, listen for answers, or a lack of answers. Can you set up a call with the child (obviously with the gatekeeping adult sitting nearby) in order to get a firsthand impression of their actual preferences?

- Do they respond to the right call-to-participate or not? If answers are shallow or do not seem right, you may need to screen them out. Trained recruiters develop a sense for professional respondents in consumer research.

- The issue is that sometimes it can be lucrative or rewarding to be a respondent, and the actual respondent may actually "sell their seat at the research table" to someone else. In some cultures, in order to avoid imposters, it is regular practice to check respondents' photo identification when they show up to participate. Are the respondents whom they say they are or are they sitting in for "the right" respondent?

5 Doing the right things

In a study, you often develop a task design, or test protocol, that describes what the respondent needs to react to and how to prompt them for responses. It is a clear source of bias if there is too wide a gap between the script and what the respondent would be doing if left to their own devices (Figure 2-8). The study must be set up in a way that bridges the respondent's realistic needs and behavior with the behavior or experience as it was intended and designed by the stakeholder.

Figure 2-8. Potential areas of bias in what respondents do during the study

Consensus bias

In a much-quoted study from 1931, pioneering social psychologists Daniel Katz, Margaret Babcock Jenness, and Floyd Henry Allport illustrated that students' estimates of the frequency that others cheat was positively correlated with their own behavior – the less you cheat, the less you expect that others will cheat. A Danish proverb can be loosely translated to a similar sentiment: *a thief thinks that everyone steals.*

Consensus bias is a common cognitive bias which describes how we – rather egocentrically – tend to believe that people will commonly share our own beliefs, values, and even behaviors. In the age of social media, this phenomenon is sometimes described using the metaphor "echo chamber," a self-explanatory term attributed to internet activist Eli Pariser circa 2010, and which refers to a filter bubble created by the content relevancy filters that we as individuals set (consciously or not) through the act of clicking on posts we are interested in, and the way algorithms on social media reinforce our choices ad libitum.

In research, this bias can (perhaps consciously, but likely unconsciously) lead researchers and stakeholders to recreate their own belief and behaviors when developing the test script. The implication is that the study will be a self-fulfilling prophecy: if you don't let the respondents' own beliefs and actions into the study, you risk running a study that revolves around itself (i.e., your bubble) and not around the audience.

In the instances where the aim of the study is to validate key hypotheses about a product or a service (e.g., if respondents understand how to use it or not), this bias goes hand in hand with the test script: you are, in effect, studying whether (or not) your concept, content, and interactions are shared with the respondents via the design. You are studying whether your echo chamber is inclusive to your audience. Taken to an extreme conclusion, this study will not tell you anything you didn't already know – it is a meaningless waste of time.

Get beyond the recency and primacy effects

This effect, also called the serial-position effect, is the tendency of a person to recall the first and last items in a series best, and the middle items worst. If one asks the children in a study to recall a list of items in any order (also called free recall), they will tend to begin recall with the end of the list, recalling those most recent items best (the recency effect). Due to the way information is stored in the brain, the first few items presented will be recalled more frequently than the middle items (the primacy effect). One simple way to adjust for this effect is to vary or even randomize the sequence or order of the stimulus between each participant. Another is to consider the speed and emphasis that is put on each item, as the children will clearly remember items better when these are presented slowly or with great emphasis than the opposite.

It is the researcher's job to make sure that the study takes its point of departure in the respondents' world – in their needs, beliefs, expectations, and behaviors. There are several ways to do this by combining ethnographical and respondent-centric approaches, and they work with both explorative and validating study approaches:

- Precede the development of a test script with observations and interviews (for instance, by capturing real-life behavior on video or in writing and replicating it in the research context).

- Pre-test the test script with domain experts from diverse backgrounds.

- Think outside your echo chamber; focus on diversity when choosing respondents and developing the script.

- Co-develop the test script together with the respondents, for example, during a pre-test interview about their past experiences, their expectations, and their daily practices.

- Let the respondents choose from a set of potential test script elements ("what would you like to do first?") rather than having a fixed set of tasks.

6 …at the right time of day or week or month

It may sound benign at first, but it is important to plan ahead to make sure that the timing of the research mimics the timing of the usage of the product or service (or the consumption of the content) that you are studying.

If the product is a toy intended to be used by a child under the supervision of an adult, the timing clearly falls during the day, perhaps even more narrowly defined as a workday afternoon or all day on weekends.

If the study aims to understand whether parents are interested in purchasing a toy, it may matter at what time of the month (relative to payday) you run the study. It may also influence the gift-givers' attitude if the study takes place shortly before or during a gift-giving season, as the gift-givers are simply more attentive toward toys during these periods.

Kids have different schedules than adults. School children are likely to have more availability to participate in research outside of school hours, perhaps in after-school activities. It may be harder to organize a session with the researcher (and observers) during after-school hours, if it falls near or after the end of a normal workday.

Typically, children often have more energy in the first half of the day – this energy swing is also common with adults but more pronounced the younger the children are. Younger kids may need their nap time. The speed of the various parts of our cognitive apparatus – our memory, our attention span, our decision-making – fluctuates throughout the day in both children and adults. This affects the timing, as well as the next item we will examine: the duration of the research.

7 …for the right duration

How long can a research session run with a child? There's no universal answer, but here are some pointers:

- Too long a duration: Testing may overly focus the kids' attention, leading to a better-than-real experience. But on the other hand, if the session drags out, the child's level of attention may decline.

- Too short: The session does not reflect the full experience, again leading to a better-than-real experience. This may be amplified if the session is short and keeps the child's level of attention higher than what is realistic.

A general recommendation is to break the script or session guide down into 15-minute-long segments and to make an assessment after each one in order to gauge if the child is able to continue to the next segment or not, and perhaps include the child in this decision. Make sure to prioritize the most important areas by putting them in the earlier segments if possible.

Be aware of the nature of the experience you are researching. If it is a fun and stimulating activity where time flies, you can likely increase the session duration compared to a more serious or strenuous activity. If the activity has a social element, running sessions with two or more respondents (e.g., friends or siblings) can save project time by having a shorter per-respondent duration; however, the social context or the possibility of group thinking may introduce various types of bias if the product is intended as a one-on-one experience.

It is always a good idea to pilot-test your script with a realistic, but tolerant, respondent to see how long it takes to go through it ahead of time, before making the appointments with actual respondents. Also, you may need to include ongoing revisions to the plan and adapt the duration if it does not fit as well as expected.

You should also consider what the realistic usage or consumption duration can be expected to be. If a product is designed for a pick-up-and-use context, the script should mimic that. In this case, you should not offer any introduction or training and this will reduce the duration of the session (all things being equal). If the product requires installing, assembly, or other time-consuming activities, consider if these can be simulated, for example, in a video clip, to cut session duration down, but in this case, be aware of any bias this shorter-than-real experience will introduce.

Lastly, but not insignificantly, is a "fly-in" time or "warm-up" time needed so that the child can relax and become comfortable with the setup and the people? If the location is familiar, and the moderator is familiar, it may take no time at all. If everything is unfamiliar to the child, consider if there are ways for the child to prepare ahead of time (e.g., by watching a video about the location, the people, and the purpose) or simply plan for 5 or 10 minutes of mutual introduction time ahead of the actual study.

8 ...in the right location/setting

The best research location with kids is not always the most comfortable for the researcher. It is where the child is comfortable, where they are familiar with the surroundings and the people and feel at home.

Figure 2-9. Potential areas of bias in what respondents do during the study

Some factors are physical, illustrated by the yellow frame in Figure 2-9:

- Kids may easily become shy if research is carried out in a corporate-looking environment, which the researcher might otherwise prefer for practical or economic reasons.

- Kids may be distracted by the decor and may even start to play with it. They may spend more energy and attention on spinning the office chair than on the product or service you are testing.

- Kids may also feel uncomfortable using furniture designed for adults, such as office tables and chairs.

Other potential stumbling blocks are psychological, illustrated by the brick-orange frame in Figure 2-9:

- They may feel awkward being under scrutiny.

- They may feel isolated if they are the only child in a room full of adults.

- They may feel uncomfortable being paired with certain other kids.

- They may be confused about their role and unsure of what is expected of them.

This is not to say that these feelings are unique to children – many adults may react the exact same way. However, the fact that children are not their own masters may add to their discomfort. Remember that they don't have the same ability to step out of an uncomfortable situation as adults have.

9 …using the right device

Often you'll need a device, like a smartphone, a tablet, a game console, a TV, or some other device, to access the content or functionality.

The right device has to be one that the respondent/child is familiar with, and the device that it is designed for and intended by the stakeholders, but when researching with children you should consider that these might not be the same. Kids often have hand-me-down smartphones or tablets, perhaps stretching several technological generations back. Developers and designers, on the other hand, often have cutting-edge equipment that likely offers a better experience. Handing the kids the newest devices to test a service or product may offer the best possible experience (and the experience more true to what kids in the future will have once their equipment has been upgraded) but it will do so at the expense of realism. Maybe the leap is not so big if the kid's device is on the same operating system (e.g., iOS or Android for smartphones and tablets) or platform (e.g., a PlayStation or Xbox), but the mere fact that the newest devices offer better experiences (sounds, graphics, response time, finish, etc.) will bias the child in favor of the experience.

If the child is using a given platform or OS for the very first time, it will likely be the platform itself – not the service or product – you're testing. That may be relevant in and of itself – you'll want to bear this in mind when analyzing the results.

A different view on the term device could include text and its readability vis-à-vis the respondent's age. Letters and numbers on a screen or a piece of paper are potentially a source of bias that can be hard for a literate adult to notice. If the child is supposed to glean information from a text, it needs to match the child's capabilities similar to the way that using the right device is important on any digital platform. A literate adult may have little or no insight into how well a 6-, 7-, or 8-year-old reads, plus literacy varies naturally from child to child. A perspective on learning the ABCs and what this requires from the child is illustrated on TV shows like *Sesame Street*.[19]

Bias during the execution phase

That's a lot of bias already, and we haven't even made it into "the field" yet! The field is the messy and treacherous real world where all of our good intentions and great plans are challenged. But fear not: the end of the list of biases is nearer!

In this phase:

- 10 Correctly primed and instructed
- 11 The right amount of priming and instruction
- 12 Correctly moderated
  - 12a Biased Questions
  - 12b Biased Answers
- 13 Monitored by the right people

10 Correctly primed and instructed

How you instruct or prime respondents will be influenced by whether you take an explorative or a validating approach to research. Exploration (e.g., what if we went in this direction?) often happens earlier in a project cycle, and its purpose – and hence the instructions given to respondents – are often more loosely defined than in studies that seek validation (e.g., how well does this work?), which often happens later in a project cycle. The exploration may be more concerned with the how and what, whereas the validation may be interested in understanding to which extent something is true or in a simple binary outcome such as yes (yes, the respondents were able to achieve something) or no (they weren't).

---

[19]There is an illustrative step-by-step breakdown here https://muppet.fandom.com/wiki/Learning_About_Letters. As a counterbalance, here's a text that points to shortcomings in the way that *Sesame Street* educates kids: https://newrepublic.com/article/123405/sesame-street, e.g., that it presents a world where "grown-ups initiate everything. And (childrens') concerns are trivial." It says that *Sesame Street's* notion of childrens' intellectual development is limited to some mechanical operations. For more critical reflections follow this link: https://en.wikipedia.org/wiki/Influence_of_Sesame_Street#Critical_reception.

To use an example from the natural world, if you run an exploration of the sea, you will look to see what is in the ocean and maybe find new sea life. If you engage in a validation, you'll check for certain species or you'll try to prove that a species lives in a certain area.

Bias is amplified if the instructions do not match the purpose. If, in an exploration, you end up with a study guide that asks mostly closed questions (e.g., does this work for you?) or deals mostly with assessing the accuracy of something (e.g., how well does this work for you?), the study will not yield an outcome to its fullest – you'll risk putting the cart before the horse, and you'll want to revise the study guide and make sure that the instructions are more open to the unknown.

Priming – the technique whereby exposure to one stimulus influences a response to a subsequent stimulus, without conscious guidance or intention – in itself is clearly a source of bias. Examples from social psychology show that exposing respondents to positive or negative stereotypes prior to a test affects their performance. Experiments by psychologists Dijksterhuis and van Knippenberg[20] established that priming the stereotype of professors on the trait "intelligent" enhanced participants' performance on a scale measuring general knowledge. Also, priming the stereotype of soccer hooligans on the trait "stupid" reduced participants' performance on a general knowledge scale.

In another priming classic, psychologists Shih, Pittinsky, and Ambady[21] primed Asian American women with either their Asian identity (stereotyped with high math ability), female identity (stereotyped with low math ability), or no priming before administering a math test. Of the three groups, Asian-primed participants performed best on the math test, and female-primed participants performed the worst.

So priming is a factor to be reckoned with. In research with kids, it can be anticipated to play a role, for instance, if a test script or other stimulus includes reminding kids of their biological age – they may perform better or worse depending on how their developmental or mental age corresponds to their biological age. Similar effects can occur if the test script focuses on their personal interests, with the positive or negative aspects of an interest possibly priming them subconsciously. This may lead them to blow their interests out of proportion – they become significantly more engaged or disengaged during the research session than if they were not primed.

---

[20]Dijksterhuis, A., & van Knippenberg, A. (1998). The relation between perception and behavior, or how to win a game of Trivial Pursuit. *Journal of Personality and Social Psychology,* 74(4), 865–877. https://doi.org/10.1037/0022-3514.74.4.865

[21]Shih, M. ,Pittinsky, T.L. , Ambady, N. (1999).Stereotype susceptibility: Identity salience and shifts in quantitative performance. *Psychological Science,* 10,80–83

Some games or toys may be culturally attributed to certain age intervals or to just one of the genders. Priming kids with these norms (e.g., this is not a toy for girls or this is a toy for younger kids) may also lead them to perform, react, or behave differently during research. In research settings, kids will often feel some level of uncertainty; perhaps they will be nervous, causing them to behave and perform below their standard. Researchers must be very careful with priming. On the one hand, they must aim to make the kids as comfortable as possible. But on the other, this may lead the kids to feel overly smothered with care and affection, and less empowered to assert and express themselves.

For researchers, it is helpful to rehearse different moderation techniques so that they can be applied swiftly in different situations, for example, if a child reacts negatively to a more affectionate moderation style or appears nervous. Also, to reduce priming it is important to give the kids a clear understanding (in brief) of the study's aim and the moderator's role ahead of time, emphasizing, for instance, that there are no right or wrong answers or actions and that the moderator is equally happy or sad if the study goes in one direction or another, as long as it follows the child's interests.

11 The right amount of priming and instruction

This step deals with the potential bias from getting too many or too few instructions. The child needs enough instructions to create a thick, rich understanding and to give substantial feedback beyond a simple "yes" or "no." But on the other hand, too many instructions may overwhelm the child, leading to confusion or boredom and a subsequent change in their behavior or preferences.

And I think that this is perhaps just the right amount of instruction for this section!

12 Correctly moderated

Moderator bias

The moderator collects the data and has a major impact on its quality.

The moderator's facial expressions, body language, tone, manner of dress, and style of language may introduce bias. Similarly, the moderator's age, social status, race, and gender can also produce bias.

Some of these influences are unavoidable, but you can control some of the physical influences. Remain as neutral as you can in dress, tone, and body language. And don't give opinions while moderating. Try to mimic the child's energy level. If the child is quiet, be quiet; if the child is loud, play along.

Figure 2-10. Biased questions

12a Biased questions

A biased question or the way you ask a question can bias the answer (Figure 2-10). Recognize and avoid your own biased questions. As a moderator, you are in control of the questions. Check your interview guide for biased questions, and rephrase them or remove them.

Here are some common biased questions found in qualitative research.

Leading question bias

Leading questions suggest what the answers should be. Putting words in respondents' mouths slants their answers.

An example of a leading question is, "Some people think that sugary candy is bad for you. Do you think so too?" Instead, frame the question neutrally: "What is your opinion about sugary candy?"

By keeping questions neutral, you reduce question bias.

Misunderstood question bias

Sometimes moderators ask questions that respondents misunderstand. Words, context, culture, and different interpretations of words and sentences can cause misunderstanding.

Simple, clear, and concrete questions reduce misunderstanding.

Unanswerable question bias

Some respondents cannot answer questions because they lack experience or reference points with a subject. For example, a specific child may not be familiar with a given toy or game, but may nonetheless try to answer questions about it. If respondents do not have experience with a product or a product category, their answers may be misinformed.

Make sure that you interview respondents with actual experience in the subject of interest when moderating qualitative research.

Metaphorically speaking

Bias from unanswerable or misunderstood questions also occurs on another cognitive level, as metaphors are not always shared between moderators and children. Moderators potentially introduce bias when they describe or explain one thing by referring to another thing through analogies (e.g., one is compared to the other, as in "this toy goes faster than lightning"), similes (e.g., one is like the other: "this toy is like a car"), and metaphors (e.g., one is the other: "this toy is a car").

Cars and lightning may actually work as reference points for most kids, but with many other metaphors you risk that kids, hearing them the first time in your study, take them literally or miss the underlying meaning altogether, for example, in expressions such as to be glued to your seat, keep your eyes peeled, lose your breath, etc.[22]

(See also the section Description bias about metaphors).

---

[22]Many more complex examples are here: www.ereadingworksheets.com/figurative-language/figurative-language-examples/metaphor-examples

Question order bias

The order that you ask the questions can introduce bias. Minimize this type of bias in qualitative research by doing the following:

- Asking general questions before specific questions
- (e.g., Would you ever play with a car? before Would you play with this car?)

- Ask open questions before closed questions
- (e.g., How would you play with this car? before Would you play with this car?)

- Asking unaided questions before aided questions
- (e.g., How would you play with a car? before How would you play with this car?)

- Asking positive questions before negative questions
- (e.g., What are some good things about this car? before What are some bad things about this car?)

- Asking behavior questions before attitude questions
- (e.g., How did you play with this car? before Did you like to play with this car?)

Diligence is necessary when ordering your topics, questions, and activities. Ask yourself if the sequence of questions causes bias due to the order in which the questions are presented. Change the order if necessary and see what makes sense.

For further information on priming, see Step 10 ("Correctly primed and instructed").

12b Biased answers

A biased answer is an untrue or partially true statement from a respondent. Bias influences and skews answers and masks the truth. An untrue statement can be intentional or unintentional. Either way it is considered bias, and it may happen for various reasons. A biased answer is, for example, a natural response to a biased question, but you should also bear in mind that the respondent takes many other factors (besides the question) into account when producing an answer, and this can encompass nearly every detail surrounding the question (Figure 2-11).

So biased answers are common, and a researcher needs to be on guard for them just as much as for the other biases in this chapter. In the following sections, I describe some common types of biased answers often found in qualitative research.

Figure 2-11. Biased answers

Cognitive overload bias

Cognitive overload describes a situation where someone, or some media (e.g., a moderator or a teacher), gives too much information or too many tasks to a person (e.g., respondents or learners) at a time, resulting in that person being unable to process the information. In this situation, the cognitive processing demands of an activity go beyond the respondent or learner's processing limits.

This is a well-known problem in usability testing, which applies the thinking-aloud protocol, where respondents are encouraged to be explicit about their thought processes while performing tasks. The mere act of thinking aloud slows down many other cognitive processes, such as inference, memory, decision-making, motor skills, or speaking. The cognitive overload bias is further amplified by the other factors that can bias a study – in particular consistency bias, which we'll take up just a few sentences from now. When the cognitive system is overloaded, the decision-making process slows down, the rate of error increases, and it becomes increasingly difficult to be consistent and to make sense of information or situations.

Several studies (and probably most parents' anecdotal evidence as well) conclude that kids perform worse (or less consistently) than adults when overloaded. For example, a 2017[23] study about task-switching concluded that children (aged 6–16) performed consistently worse and were more susceptible to task manipulation than adults (18–27 years old). Another study from 2011[24] found that younger children (grades 1–2) perform more poorly than older children (grades 6–7) or adults (college students) on tests of working memory.

This means that research with kids (unless, of course, it is a study about cognitive overload) should be very mindful of the research setup and adapt it specifically to the children's developmental stage and cognitive limitations. This means that the younger the kids, the fewer the number of "moving parts" that should be introduced: there should be less stimuli, fewer and simpler tasks, less switching between tasks, less instruction, less moderation, and an economy of language that uses fewer and simpler words.

Consistency bias

Respondents try to appear consistent in their answers. This happens, for instance, in a test or interview, when a person's previous statement influences later statements, even if one of the statements is untrue. For example, a respondent may say that they perform a certain task in a certain way or have a certain preference, and then during the course of the test realize that, in fact, that was not correct, but in order to remain consistent, they proceed unhindered rather than correct their position.

Consistency is different between different age groups – the strive for consistency is less pronounced and less evident among younger children. Regardless of the respondent's age, if a response does not seem right, simply ask for a clarification – at least you will know if there is an inconsistency and you can include this in your analysis.

---

[23]Consistent Performance Differences between Children and Adults Despite Manipulation of Cue-Target Variables by Jessie-Raye Bauer, et al. (2017) www.ncbi.nlm.nih.gov/pubmed/?term=Bauer%20JR%5BAuthor%5D&cauthor=true&cauthor_uid=28824489
[24]Age Differences in Visual Working Memory Capacity: Not Based on Encoding Limitations by Nelson Cowan et al. (2011) www.ncbi.nlm.nih.gov/pmc/articles/PMC3177168/

Dominant respondent bias

When you engage more than one respondent at a time (e.g., in a focus group or when interviewing a group of siblings or friends), sometimes (or even most times) you will encounter dominant respondents. They can influence other respondents. Dominant respondents will dominate talk time, leveraging their knowledge, expertise, energy, attractiveness, and charisma to make them dominant, just as they would in other social settings. This also happens with group sessions with younger children.

To reduce bias, keep dominant respondents in check by making sure that other respondents get equal time to think and speak.

Error bias

Respondents are not always right; sometimes they make mistakes. Memories fade, and people forget. As a researcher, you will need to check if respondents' behavior supports or contradicts what they say, and cross check your data and findings. For example, in a test with tasks, you cannot simply rely on the respondents to self-report their performance. Ironically, the error bias can also go the other way: respondents may report errors that were, in fact, not errors.

This type of error bias should not be confused with the fact that errors occur – and occur regularly – in research with children, and that these errors may themselves be important findings (e.g., the errors reveal that the kids are struggling to perform a certain task, perhaps because the design or user interface is faulty in some way). You should set your study up in a way that will tell you if there is a true error – not just indicate what the respondents believe is an error.

Hostility bias

Some respondents may be angry with the moderator, stakeholder, or sponsor and provide negative responses as a result. Keep your cool. Continue to ask questions; however, if the hostility persists or pollutes the data, break off the interview. A snack break might perhaps help reduce feelings of hostility in the child and lead to more engagement. Hostility can also be a sign of low blood sugar, or of confusion or stress – all of which are excellent grounds either for taking a break or for postponing or cancelling the session.

On the other hand, hostility can sometimes be a reaction to consider in itself. For instance, if a product, brand, or message evokes an unintended hostile response, you may consider it a finding rather than a source of bias, depending on your perspective. It can suggest changes or redesigns to the product or service, the branding, or the message.

Moderator acceptance bias (acquiescence or confirmation bias)

Sometimes respondents provide answers simply to please the moderator. Respondents interpret what they believe the moderator wants to hear, and thus their answers may be false. Acquiescence bias (also known as the friendliness bias or "yea-saying") is common in research. You'll notice it when a respondent shows a tendency to agree with whatever it is that you're asking or stating. This is human nature: some people have inherently acquiescent personalities and are more likely to agree with statements than disagree, regardless of the content. Sometimes people – and especially children – perceive the moderator (an adult) as an authority or expert, which makes them more likely to react positively to a question.

Acquiescence is sometimes the path of least resistance for a respondent – an "easy way out" – as it takes less time and effort than it would to take each of the options into careful consideration. Sometimes kids are impatient and will simply agree just so they may complete a task or study as fast as possible.

If you as a moderator feel that the answers don't ring true, challenge them in a friendly way. At the same time, try not to reveal too much about yourself and any predispositions you might have (see also Step 10 "Correctly primed and instructed").

Mood bias

When respondents are in an extreme mood state – overly happy or sad, energetic or lethargic – they may provide answers that reflect their mood. Similarly, certain personality traits manifest themselves even in young children: angry or negative people provide angry or pessimistic answers. Similarly, impatient kids may provide short, curt, hurried answers.

Again, perhaps a snack and/or a break will change the mood for the better.

As a researcher, you will likely mentally prepare for a research session by putting on your "game face," by assuming your researcher persona – the version of you that is attentive, approachable, professional, polite and, hence, positive, and perhaps even cheerful.

But compare this standard researcher mood to, for example, a tired, grumpy respondent (but not too tired and grumpy to participate in the session) and consider how you can reach the best outcome of the session. Perhaps changing your attitude to a similar level of grumpiness will work best. Or perhaps staying cheerful will lead to better results. Or perhaps a middle ground somewhere between the two is what's needed. (Cancelling the session altogether is of course also an option.) The imbalance of cheerful vs. grumpy may be a larger impediment to harvesting data than the more balanced grumpy vs. grumpy mood set, since the grumpy respondent may become even more grumpy when faced with encouragement from a cheerful moderator. From my personal experience as a moderator, I find that my natural response is to try to adapt my mood and energy level to that of the respondent, meaning that I'll tone it down when the respondent is quiet so as to invite the respondent to fill the space as much as they wish, and turn up my voice and overall responsiveness when the respondent is boisterous, loud, challenging, or even confrontational in their attitude. In this way, I invite the respondent to feel comfortable with the situation. Your best option as a researcher is to check for mood state and continually assess the answers you get.

Overstatement bias

Sometimes respondents overstate their intentions or opinions. It happens, for example, as a result of priming – for instance, if a certain affinity (such as being a fan of a certain team or product) or affiliation (e.g., belonging to a social group) is highlighted or enforced in an early part of the study (see also Step 10 "Correctly primed and instructed").

However, overstatement can also occur if the child feels that the moderator needs extra persuasion, for instance, if the moderator does not react (or does not react sufficiently) to the child's statement or behavior and the child then decides to try to "dial it up a notch." In these ways overstatement bias works in a similar way as error bias: if it is not recognized by the respondent (unintentional and unaware) it can be a finding in itself, but if it is intentional, it is a source of bias.

As a researcher, you need to be attuned to overstatements and recognize and moderate them – if not during the session, then at least in the analysis phase.

Reference bias (order bias)

During a research session, respondents develop a frame of reference from a previous question, discussion, activity or thought. They carry this reference on to the next question, which biases their answers. The very sequence of stimuli, topics, questions, and activities produces this reference bias.

You can reduce reference bias in qualitative research by logically ordering questions, topics, and activities. A logical order will often follow a straightforward chronology and will weigh each step carefully and equally, avoiding overemphasis and underexposure.

When you have a smaller or larger group of respondents, in focus groups, for example, you can reduce the influence respondents may have on one another by asking them to write down or draw their reactions before talking about them.

Reference bias is especially challenging to a researcher when the purpose of the study is to determine how much explanation is required from a message or a product. For instance, if you produce three versions or a product – one with little explanation, one with a great deal, and one in-between – you will need to randomize the order between respondents. Because of this, you will likely require three times as many respondents compared with research for a single message or product. In their experience with a first product variation, respondents will learn things which will inevitably influence their encounters with other product variations and thus lead to biased results.

Sensitive issue bias

During the study you may touch upon sensitive topics, about which respondents would rather not talk. In such instances, respondents may give false answers in order to hide secrets or avoid the sensitive topics altogether. It may not initially be clear which topics may be sensitive to children, so researchers may want to clarify this as soon as possible – for instance, through desk research and interviews with caregivers and specialists.

If you find that an issue is sensitive, you'll need to build a firmer and more trusting relationship than usual. Kids will be more likely to speak with others if they sense the atmosphere is positive and trusting. Another strategy is to use projective techniques and indirect questions (e.g., what would kids your age think? or someone like you, what would they think?).

Social acceptance bias

Respondents sometimes provide answers that are socially acceptable but false; they will say one thing even though they may feel or think something else (Figure 2-12). They may twist the truth, or offer half-truths. Most people – adults and children alike – want to conform to their group and can find it uncomfortable to step outside of the norms and standards. Nevertheless, it is clearly a robust source of bias if you can't rely on respondents' feedback.

Figure 2-12. Social acceptance bias

As a researcher you may want to challenge these kinds of answers tactfully. You can use projective techniques or indirect questions (see section "Sensitive issue bias").

Sponsor bias

When respondents know who is sponsoring the research, their feelings and opinions about the sponsor may bias answers. Kids may have an endless and vocal love for a certain toy, or they may associate a certain brand with toys for a different age group or gender than themselves.

As much as possible try not to reveal the name of the sponsor. Keep your studies "blind" as long as you can in qualitative research. If, for instance, you wish to limit the exposure of the sponsor brand, you can add stimuli from other similar brands to your study.

The most dreaded answer: "I don't know."

Kids will answer "I don't know" at a higher frequency in research than adults, and there are many reasons why.

One is that they simply don't know. Knowing implies a certainty, knowledge, awareness, and consciousness that comes with age and experience and with status – in fact, in most areas of their lives, kids rely on adults to know stuff.

So even if the kid actually does know, they may not feel that they are allowed to express this or are unable to do so. Not knowing can also mean not knowing the right words for an opinion or experience – that you don't know the words to express what you, in fact, do know deep down.

Another is fatigue – the child cannot summon the energy needed to come up with a reply. An adult respondent who has experience from being exposed to a broader range of situations may need less energy to come up with an answer, or feel more compelled or obliged to answer, due to the shared social norms among adults.

A third reason is indifference or a realization on the child's part that there is nothing for them to gain in this section of the study. They have resigned themselves, and "I don't know" actually means "I don't care" or "I don't want to know."

A fourth reason is confusion – for instance, if the question is about something they have not yet formed an opinion on. When asked whether they like or prefer something, perhaps over some alternative, replying "I don't know" may actually mean "I don't like." This is different from the three previous reasons for not knowing (not knowing a fact, not having the energy to answer, or not caring about it) in that the child may be unfamiliar with the experience of something (rather than the facts about that thing), and thus they don't know if they like it or not.

A fifth reason is that they don't feel that they have the time to come up with an answer. The child may feel that processing the question and considering relevant responses will take some time and they have not yet reached any conclusions. Perhaps they sense that there's no resolution in sight. So, on the one hand, they are being polite and letting you proceed with your study but, on the other, they may in fact be able to answer coherently at a later point – perhaps even very soon (…or perhaps not). The point is that they don't know right now. As a moderator, you need to communicate clearly so that the child can understand your priorities – perhaps you actually prioritize that they will spend time on the answer because the answer is important to you.

Adult moderators may become surprised or annoyed by frequent "I don't know" replies and may feel that kids use it as an easy way out of a situation, but moderators must remember that they put the child in the situation, not the other way around. The kids may say "I don't know," which is more polite than 'This is boring" or "I feel like you're wasting my time" or "I would much rather be playing."

Angela Watson is a teacher, whose blog, *The cornerstone for teachers*,[25] provides the following useful ideas for responding to children who respond that they don't know. Most, if not all, are also relevant in a research context too. Generally speaking, these involve following up with topic-specific questions that provide some of the missing information or vocabulary that the child needs in order to put the pieces of the puzzle together. Variations on this include

- *I understand you don't know. What would you say if you did know?*
- *What part do you know for sure?*
- *Pretend you had a choice of answers: which one would you pick?*
- *What would be your best guess if you did know?*
- *What are the possibilities?*
- *If you did have an idea, what would it be?*

In addition to this, sometimes parents are available during the study, and they can often provide valuable assistance in helping a child to loosen up, as parents will normally know of ways to help their child communicate more effectively.

13 Monitored by the right people

The right observers are those who care about the research findings and can do something with them afterward – they can decide or design something based upon the results. Observers can potentially glean invaluable information from a research session – their mere presence and firsthand exposure to the audience can be both rare and useful.

There's a risk that your study may be biased by the presence of the wrong observers. For example, stakeholders who have already made up their minds, or who have a vested interest in a given outcome, may seek to influence you or other researchers. Another group of observers are those who, rather than listening in on the sessions, view the presence of other stakeholders as an opportunity to start discussions and devote their attention to topics other than the actual research. Yet another group of observers are those who witness only a fraction of the sessions and then form a strong opinion that now "they've seen it all."

---

[25]https://thecornerstoneforteachers.com/bright-idea-responding-kids-say-dont-know/

Observers often struggle to get a clear view of the respondent and their interactions, and this is accentuated if the respondent interacts with smaller objects such as products or smartphones. If they need to move up closer to the child, the child may feel crowded and intimidated, and their responses may be inhibited. Providing cameras and screen mirroring can sometimes mitigate this.

As the researcher, it is also your role to manage any observers and their expectations, maybe through verbal instructions or even a written code of conduct.

Related to this type of bias, but of a completely different nature, is that of upcoming respondents (e.g., siblings, classmates, or friends of the respondent) who may unintentionally be within eyeshot or earshot of the ongoing session. They will be biased by having heard the questions and the replies from others. This will have taught or shown them things or ideas that will change the way they will experience these same things or ideas during their research session.

Bias during the analysis and reporting phase

In this phase:

14 A rigorous, methodical analysis

15 A timely, relevant, and actionable report

16 A simple and focused presentation

17 Sustaining the findings

18 Actioned right

14 A rigorous, methodical analysis

Analyzed right means applying a researcher mindset with rigor and method – not just looking at some of the research data or looking at it haphazardly.

By qualitative data, I refer to nonnumerical information such as interview transcripts, notes, video and audio recordings, images, and texts. It may include drawings or other materials that the kids produced before or during the session. (However, we sometimes combine quantitative and qualitative approaches – see the "The one score to rule them all" section in Chapter 4.) The data is analyzed for its content, narrative, discourse, thematic framework, or semantics. More recently, Grounded Theory has grown in influence: in this approach you start with an analysis of a single case in order to formulate a hypothesis (called a theory in the Grounded Theory framework). Then you look at additional cases to see if they contribute to the hypothesis (theory).

In contrast to quantitative methods, qualitative data analysis really has no universally applicable techniques that can generate findings. The analytical and critical thinking skills of the researcher play a significant role in data analysis in qualitative studies. Therefore, a second qualitative study cannot be expected to generate precisely the same results.

Part of the analysis is to identify common themes, patterns, and relationships within the behavior and responses of your respondent group (Figure 2-13). The researcher looks for word and phrase repetitions, perhaps expressed with unusual emotions, and compares their findings with those of other researchers, perhaps through a literature review. What respondents said – or didn't say – in relation to what they were expected to say is considered, as are metaphors and analogies, which can relate the study to others in different areas and uncover similarities and differences between them.

Figure 2-13. The analysis can consist of Post-it collages (and have their own particular type of beauty)

15 A timely, relevant, and actionable report

By reporting, I often mean a written product – a document or presentation, or perhaps an email if in a hurry – but it can also be a prototype, a video, an audio recording, a drawing or even a theatrical presentation or reenactment. If fact, a written report – rigid, comprehensive, detailed, in a long format – may be exactly what the intended audience (stakeholders, designers, developers, project managers, etc.) is *least* interested in. A more involved report takes longer to produce, but perhaps the project is in a hurry and your precious and precise findings may be obsolete if you deliver them after the stakeholders' deadline. So reported right means reported in a *timely, relevant, and actionable* manner.

Old-school researchers (such as yours truly) will also likely mention the *Common Industry Format for Usability Test Reports* issued by NIST[26] (The National Institute of Standards and Technology in the United States) as a source of inspiration for what a report can include (although it has not been updated since 2001).

Biased reporting

Moderators and analysts sometimes produce bias as a side effect of reporting the results of qualitative research. Keeping an open mind requires extraordinary discipline. Experiences, beliefs, feelings, wishes, attitudes, views, errors, and references, as well as culture, state of mind, and personality, can bias analysis and reporting. Both the conscious and subconscious minds are at work when reporting. Moderators and analysts are, like anyone else, fallible human beings. However, having a researcher mindset means striving for maximum impartiality, letting the data (rather than preconceptions) guide your reasoning, explicitly pointing to your own deductions and conclusions, and keeping an open mind and always seeking alternative conclusions.

It helps to have more than one analyst. Having two people analyze the data means that you'll get two different perspectives. If one analyst subconsciously skews the reporting, the other may spot it.

In addition, you can have respondents review your findings, but this may prove difficult if you are dealing with young children.

Positive reporting bias and publication bias

An interesting side effect of doing something meaningful, such as research, is that – as you get invested in it – you may be biased toward producing a meaningful outcome. You don't want all your work to be in vain; you expect that it will lead to something positive. When reporting a study, a researcher must be wary of publication bias, which occurs when the outcome or results of the study influence the decision of whether to publish or otherwise distribute the findings.

---

[26]https://tsapps.nist.gov/publication/get_pdf.cfm?pub_id=151449

The interesting part of this bias is "the file-drawer problem" described by NASA research astrophysicist Jeffrey D. Scargle.[27] Researchers leave those results that came out with reaffirmations of old insights or produced no findings at all – something that no one is interested in – in the drawer. The unpublished results are imagined to be tucked away in drawers in researchers' file cabinets. The result is, simply put, that if we only ever publish those studies that produce new insights or have an outcome, our impression and expectation will be that every study must or will have an outcome. The researchers will be aiming to find something publishable rather than letting the study unfold – whether spectacular or not.[28]

16 A simple and focused presentation

The Chinese whisper game (also known as "telephone") is a party game in which one person whispers a message to the person next to them and the story is then passed progressively to several others, with inaccuracies accumulating as the game goes on (Figures 2-14 and 2-15). The last person in the row has to say the message out loud and it can be very amusing to compare it with the original message.

---

[27] Journal of Scientific Exploration, Vol. 14, No. 1, pp. 91–106, 2000, www.scientificex-ploration.org/docs/14/jse_14_1_scargle.pdf

[28] In sciences that produce a lot of quantitative research, such as astrophysics, the result of Publication Bias is also that, if researchers only publish results that show a significant finding, it disturbs the balance of findings as a whole, and inserts bias in favor of positive results.

Figure 2-14. The Chinese whisper game – a metaphor for how report findings live on – Step one. (In this case illustration of the Chinese whisper game, I am wearing a scuba tank for some reason.)

I sometimes think of the Chinese whisper game when I report findings. I am the first person in the row, handing down the message, and part of the researcher's job is to try to limit the amount of noise and distortion that goes into the message as it travels into the stakeholders' (and sometimes the stakeholders' stakeholders') realm. Though easier said than done, effective communication is crucial when presenting research findings. You should strive to keep the message as simple as possible, provide explicit key takeaways, and keep the report focused on predetermined areas (e.g., the initial purpose and objectives of the study).

Figure 2-15. The Chinese whisper game – Step two

Additionally, several mundane considerations present themselves, such as trying to avoid misunderstandings, giving adequate context for the results, and being aware of technical caveats in the findings. It may be helpful to think about the presentation as the culmination of a research project, as something to be very careful and deliberate about: you can prepare, run, and report a fantastic study, but this can all be for naught if it falls short in the presentation.

Hindsight bias

Sometimes when you present findings, you'll hear stakeholders say, "We knew this already" or "That's nothing new," but somehow this knowledge was not available or present at the onset of the study. Don't let this fool you – hindsight bias is very common.

Psychologists Baruch Fischhoff and Ruth Beyth demonstrated this bias in *I Knew It Would Happen: Remembered Probabilities of Once-Future Things*[29] with their findings of a study in 1975 during the Nixon presidency. People close to the president had predicted the likelihood of various possible outcomes of

---

[29]www.researchgate.net/publication/223213727_I_Knew_It_Would_Happen_ Remembered_Probabilities_of_Once-Future_Things

President Nixon's trips to Peking and Moscow in 1972, and the researchers asked them later, and without warning, to remember their own predictions (or to reconstruct them, in the event that they had forgotten). The study concluded that the subjects seldom perceived having been very surprised by what had or had not happened – in essence they recalled their predictions as being more accurate than they really were.[30]

Clearly this bias can occur in any kind of study – regardless of the respondents' age – so long as there are stakeholders associated with the study.

A positive aspect of this bias is that, if your presentation evoked an "I knew it!" reaction, it can be attributed to the relevancy of the findings of the research and – clearly – their resonance with your key stakeholders. Which is no small thing.

17 Sustaining the findings

I have included this step in order to highlight something that is implied in the previous steps about the reporting and presenting of findings: namely, that often a study's findings will continue to live on in the stakeholders' realm. If you consider an impactful study with many succinct findings, it may be a good use of your and your research colleagues' time to implement features or processes that will sustain the life of these findings. To build upon the Chinese whisper game metaphor, you may want to inject the primary storyteller into the middle of the row of whisperers in order to monitor the distortion and correct the narrative (Figure 2-16).

---

[30]The outcome for the United States was an improved relationship with China, which over time opened a gap between China and the Soviet Union. In addition, important nuclear arms control agreements were signed with the USSR. (https://en.wikipedia.org/wiki/Richard_Nixon%27s_1972_visit_to_China)

Figure 2-16. The Chinese whisper game, Step three. (Still clad in my diver's gear, I sustain the message down the line.)

18 Actioned right

We've arrived at our destination. We, the researchers, have handed over the findings to designers, developers, decision-makers, and other stakeholders, and now it is up to them to take action. It would be sad if they did not. It would be even sadder if they did the opposite of our recommendations. Few full-time researchers have the opportunity (or sometimes the inclination) to follow up on, or influence the actions taken by, stakeholders at later points in the development process.

But this is the bigger picture of research and bias – neither comes out of nothing and neither becomes anything by itself. The 18 steps will not always go right – it may be two steps forward and one step backward. You may not arrive at any destination at all. Great research doesn't happen by mistake or by chance, but through rigor, process, hard work, and careful scrutiny of your own practices. And to paraphrase Yoda, by learning from one's failures.

Bias is not a bug – it's a feature

To be fair (and because it is rather interesting and relevant to this chapter as well!), bias is very helpful to human cognition in many ways – actually it is crucial to our functioning as human beings. When we are faced with complex or dynamic situations with multitudes of options, or when we need to make decisions fast – when the world throws things at us – we rely on our past experiences and what they have taught us – whether it is the laws and realities of physics, of society, or of our own selves. We make predictions on what scenarios and outcomes are most likely, we weigh them and we choose between them. The more certain we feel about our assessment, the faster we arrive at a conclusion. Biases such as prejudice and stereotyping allows us a cognitive shortcut in our decision-making.

Research into bias itself is frequent in neuroscience and social psychology[31] and it suggests that bias provides us with many advantages. Bias may lead us not to follow facts but rather to trust our "gut feeling" and go against our better judgment. Bias lets us scrutinize options and select a target or focal point (whether physical or mental) to focus on first, instead of freezing and becoming overwhelmed by input. Bias helps us develop a rapid and practical response in situ, instead of coming up with a possibly more optimal long-term solution. It cuts through the clutter of information and helps us to make sense of it by building and maintaining categories, genres, and mental models. Bias also allows us the headspace to explore and complete more problem-solving that we might otherwise have had to abandon too early. Through evolution, bias has helped humans to think and act faster, to be self-protective and selfish, but also at the same time empathetic and social. In research we must strive to achieve a similar balance and to coexist with bias. This chapter hopefully will remind researchers to address the bias they don't know, and keep on doing so throughout the process. Better the bias you know than the bias you don't.

Further reading on bias

Humans have cultivated biases down through the generations. And vice-versa: certain biases may have been relevant and useful in the Stone Age or the Middle Ages but may have changed or ceased as societies developed. Our biases are not a mishap of evolution: our bodies evolved and adapted to perform specific tasks, and so did our brains. Following that line of thought, bias is not something we can separate ourselves from. We *are* our biases; we are our reasonings – as perfect or flawed as they may be.

---

[31]For example, www.ncbi.nlm.nih.gov/pubmed/10580317

The term *cognitive bias* is associated with Daniel Kahneman and Amos Tversky and their studies of behavioral economics in the early 1970s. Their research looked at apparent anomalies and contradictions in human behavior. In particular, they found that people, when offered a choice formulated in one way, might display risk aversion but, when offered essentially the same choice formulated in a different way, might display risk-seeking behavior. In 2002 Kahneman was awarded the Nobel Prize in Economic Sciences[32] and in 2012 he published *Thinking, Fast and Slow*,[33] which stoked interest in behavioral science.

The biases I've described here affect how children behave as respondents as well as how adults conceive, plan, execute, moderate, and report findings from studies with children, but bias clearly has consequences beyond user research.[34] All of the cognitive biases described in Wikipedia (as of 2016) have been beautifully and artfully arranged and designed by John Manoogian III ("jm3"), with the categories and descriptions originally by Buster Benson.[35] It is available as a poster if you are interested.[36] I was (and still am!) and now it hangs in my office and attracts a bit of attention from my colleagues.

You are now at the end of the bias chapter, but if you are thirsty for more, there is a comprehensive list of the most relevant biases in behavioral economics (there are currently 40 of them).[37] Not all the biases are specifically applicable to the research situation per se, but they are relevant to the decision-making process[38] and thus are highly relevant in that respect.

---

[32] https://en.wikipedia.org/wiki/List_of_Nobel_Memorial_Prize_laureates_in_Economics

[33] Published by Farrar, Straus and Giroux: https://en.wikipedia.org/wiki/Thinking,_Fast_and_Slow

[34] For example in clinical research: a group of health researchers in the UK maintain a Catalog of Bias here: https://catalogofbias.org/about/

[35] Buster Benson wrote "Why are we yelling – a new framework that frees you from the futility of unproductive conflict and pointless arguments" (2019) – I heard him read it on Audible and learned a lot. His blog, Buster's wobbly rickshaw, is here: https://buster.substack.com/

[36] https://commons.wikimedia.org/wiki/File:The_Cognitive_Bias_Codex_-_180%2B_biases,_designed_by_John_Manoogian_III_(jm3).png

[37] Find it at https://thedecisionlab.com/biases/

[38] According to the site, humans make around 35,000 decisions per day, which makes me wonder how they count that kind of thing, especially since our brains are largely unchanged since the Stone Age.

Succeed Through Better Research Practice

This chapter offers a list of practices – advice, concerns, considerations – that may inspire you to improve and help you produce better research results.

Compliance to rules and regulations

Compared to research with adults, in research with children there is even more focus on GDPR[1] (General Data Protection Regulation, if you're in the European Union) and the COPPA regulations (Children's Online Privacy Protection Act, in the United States). This section points you to three main

---

[1] The General Data Protection Regulation (GDPR) is a legal framework that sets guidelines for the collection and processing of personal information from individuals who live in the European Union (EU).

© Thomas Visby Snitker 2021

T. V. Snitker, *User Research with Kids*, https://doi.org/10.1007/978-1-4842-7071-4_3

international sources, but there is likely also local or national legislation governing research with children in your area or the area you will be studying. In Denmark, for instance, a broad range of public authorities, NGOs, associations, and private institutions are obliged under Danish law to vet prospective employees and volunteers who are in regular contact with children. Holders of a Børneattest (children's certificate) have been verified to have no criminal history of sexual abuse.

The UN adopted the Convention on the Rights of the Child in 1989.[2] It lists 12 rights and establishes that childhood is separate from adulthood, and lasts until 18 years old; "it is a special, protected time, in which children must be allowed to grow, learn, play, develop and flourish with dignity." The Convention went on to become the most widely ratified human rights treaty in history and has helped transform children's lives.

At the basis of the Convention are the following three statements that should also be observed when researching with children:

- Children and young people have the same general human rights as adults and also specific rights that recognize their special needs.

- Children are neither the property of their parents nor are they helpless objects of charity.

- They are human beings and are the subject of their own rights.

GDPR (General Data Protection Regulation)

In short, the GDPR[3] sets out principles for the lawful processing of personal data, which includes the collection, organization, structuring, storage, alteration, consultation, use, communication, combination, restriction, erasure, or destruction of personal data. As a researcher, GDPR means that you'll need to comply with the following.

A consent form

This is a form that you produce at the beginning of a study, along with a respondent profile description or a recruitment screener. The consent form walks potential respondents through what data the researcher wants to collect and how, where, and why that data will be used. The participant (e.g., the parent, teacher, or guardian) must read the consent form, manually check

---

[2]Find it here: www.ohchr.org/en/professionalinterest/pages/crc.aspx
[3]https://ico.org.uk/for-organisations/guide-to-data-protection/guide-to-the-general-data-protection-regulation-gdpr/

the "I agree" boxes themselves on behalf of the child, and provide a signature to confirm that they have consented to data processing. You need to save this form and store it together with any additional data from that particular session (e.g., video recordings) in a way that makes it easy for you to retrieve it, should the respondent wish to withdraw their consent at a later point.

Minimize the collection of unnecessary information

Talk with your stakeholders about what sort of information you definitely need to collect and store from the project. Video recordings are a good example of something you could discuss: how likely is it that anyone will ever review them? Do any team members have concrete plans for reviewing them? If not, then perhaps video recordings are not actually necessary for the project.

Ensure that all user data (including data used by third-party tools) is being stored and processed securely

If you are storing and processing the data yourself (or in your immediate department), you can probably better vouch for the security than for a third-party contributor, such as an email or survey program like SurveyMonkey or MailChimp. Nevertheless, in order to comply with GDPR you need to ensure security for every step that the user's data passes through.

Give users control of their data

You are obliged to tell your users (again, the parent, teacher, or guardian) why you are collecting the data, what you are doing with it, and how long you are keeping it. This means that

- If a user requests it, you are obligated to give them a copy of all the data that you have collected about them.

- If a user says that their data is inaccurate, you must correct it. (This implies that you'll need to be able to find the data, so you'll need to know how to store it in the first place.)

- If a user requests it, you are obligated to stop processing their data.

- If a user requests it, you must delete all their data.

- If the user would like to move from your service to another service, you must allow them to transfer their data out of your service in a machine-readable format.

- In most cases, you are required to process any of these user requests within one month.

These are the main rules for research, but there are plenty of other rules if, for instance, you use the data for marketing or machine learning.

COPPA (Children's Online Privacy Protection Act)

The Children's Online Privacy Protection Act "imposes certain requirements on operators of websites or online services directed to children under 13 years of age."[4] This is especially relevant if you recruit, interview, and/or interact with young respondents online. In essence, for researchers, COPPA works in the same way as GDPR. (However, if you operate a website for children, it is a very different kettle of fish.)

ESOMAR Codes and Guidelines

Also highly relevant to researchers working with children are the *ESOMAR Codes and Guidelines for Interviewing Children and Young People*.[5] ESOMAR stands for European Society for Opinion and Market Research, and it is a nonprofit organization that promotes ethical and professional guidance in research. The guidelines help sensitize researchers to the precarious and specific nature of research with children and young people of any age. It also has an explicit success criterion that is worth mentioning here: "A key criterion must always be that when the parent or other person responsible for the child hears about the content or circumstances of the interview, no reasonable person would expect him or her to be upset or disturbed."[6]

Best practice

This section aims to supplement the previous chapters with tips and tricks from my research practice. With the aim of making them useful and practical, I've organized them into three research project stages: preparation, execution, and reporting.

---

[4]www.ftc.gov/enforcement/rules/rulemaking-regulatory-reform-proceedings/childrens-online-privacy-protection-rule
[5]https://www.esomar.org/uploads/public/knowledge-and-standards/codes-andguidelines/ESOMAR_Codes-and-Guidelines_Interviewing-Children-and-Young-People.pdf
[6]www.esomar.org/uploads/public/knowledge-and-standards/codes-and-guide-lines/ESOMAR Codes-and-Guidelines Interviewing-Children-and-Young-

Prepare for best practice

1. Plan your session and design the research context with the child's capabilities and interests at heart. Make sure that the child's safety and comfort are higher on the priority list than convenient location and timing for you and your stakeholders.

2. If possible, arrange the study to take place in a location that is familiar for the respondents, such as their home or school.

3. If you host the session or rent a venue, decorate the research location in a child-friendly way, check if the furniture is comfortable for a child, and make sure the location is tolerant to children's natural behavior (e.g., that it is easy to clean up if there's a spill, if there is room enough for kids to run around and blow off a little steam, that cords and wire are not lying around across the floor or near delicate furniture that can easily be knocked over). Plan where any accompanying adults or children will be during the session (e.g., within eye- or earshot, or in a nearby room). Avoid swiveling office chairs (they are hard for kids to sit still in) and obvious nearby distractions (e.g., a TV set showing a kids show or toys that are not meant to be played with).

4. Consider what will be the simplest setup possible for soliciting feedback from the kids. Limit instructions (both verbal and, in particular, written instructions), limit stimulus materials, limit the number of distractions at the location, limit the number of observers, limit the session length, and keep the number of gadgets and devices to a minimum.

5. Leave time and resources for a pilot test without kids: a session or two where the moderators test the flow, the stimuli, and the questions for real, but with one or more adult respondents. In order to provide you with a sobering look at how much material you can actually cover during the allotted session interval, when you recruit pilot testers, skew toward some that are

   a. Tolerant (e.g., if your system or process breaks down, tolerant respondents will allow you more margin for error – they will not break down too)

b. Someone with no other agenda than to "test the test" (so not a stakeholder such as a designer, developer, or other person with a stake in the outcome)

6. To supplement a question guide, consider drafting a play guide or a story guide that invites the child to tell a story involving the elements and topics at hand.

7. Consider if it makes sense for kids to make a drawing of their experience. If so, remember to bring drawing paper and colored pencils and set aside plenty of time for this activity.

8. Consider if it makes sense to include physical objects (tangibles) whose sole purpose is to serve as conversation starters and to assist the child in explaining their thoughts. If your research includes making comparisons, choosing between different versions, or taking decisions, objects may also prove useful and conducive for the children.

9. In your question guide try to use open-ended questions as much as possible. Consider following up on yes/no questions with comprehension checks (e.g., *How did you understand this question?*).

10. In your question guide, use straightforward language with words and metaphors suitable to the child's age group.

Research and report using best practice

1. Provide snacks and drinks that are approved by the parents and other stakeholders. Perhaps start the session with a snack break and an opportunity to use the bathroom.

2. The connection between the moderator and the child is crucial to the outcome. Establish a relationship by doing something together and by chit-chatting with the respondent, but notice that kids are not as trained in the arts and customs of small talk as adults are and will take the conversation seriously. A warm-up exercise is also an option. Even the small trip made together from the reception point to the research point can serve as an icebreaker.

3. The initial greeting to the child should remind them that they are not being evaluated, quizzed, or tested – that the purpose is to generate ideas for future developments, and that in the session there are no right or wrong answers, no stupid questions, and no judgment.

4. As a moderator, it can be hard to come up with the right response, encouragement, or question in the middle of a session.

   As a supplement to your question guide or test script, build yourself a library of standard answers or standard probes that are relevant to the specific study and to the respondent's age group; decide in advance what you'll say if the child is bored, hesitant, snarky, hungry, or confused.

5. Decide in advance how much assistance and guidance it is advisable for the moderator to give and how they should give it.

6. Decide in advance what to do with parents or accompanying adults and other children. Are they observers, are they part of the session, or are they completely separated from the study (e.g., in another room)? Make this arrangement explicit to everyone in the session. The adult may be a valuable resource of information or co-moderation in some cases, but a distraction in other cases.

7. This may sound trivial, but moderators must make sure to pay attention to what the child replies, for instance, if you ask for their favorite activities, or if they have siblings, or how their day has been so far. This is just one of many ways you can show that you take them and their replies seriously.

8. Be as honest and realistic in your feedback with the child as possible. Don't overpraise their performance, but do be supportive. Don't make them out to be more special than they are – they are likely very special but not super-duper extra special. They will likely see right through any pretence on the part of the moderator.

9. Consider if you can run parallel research sessions with other children in the vicinity so that each individual respondent feels more comfortable by being around other kids.

However, make sure that upcoming respondents who are waiting in the vicinity don't get to see or hear the stimulus or the questions.

Also remember the more than 15 potential biases just in the research-execution phase alone that we examined in Chapter 2.

10. Consider not that you will produce a report that will be the most precise or the most attractive or the fastest, but rather the most impactful. It will need to balance all three of these attributes – precision, attractiveness, and speed – and this balance will change from project to project. A report that is imprecise and ugly, but fast, may be more impactful and deliver more value to the team who needs it and needs it now.

Remember the metaphor of the Chinese whisper game from Chapter 2? Perhaps it is helpful to think about your position at the front of this long line of "listening whisperers" and how your message will make it through to the end unscathed. What is the best mix of timeliness, precision, and aesthetics for your report and the message it contains?

11. Do you need to share video and/or photographic material featuring child respondents? Assuming that you already have the necessary permissions in place, be mindful of not relaying any personal information about them.

Perhaps you aren't able to produce any video material that is meaningful without disclosing some measure of personal information – it may actually be more trouble than it's worth to include video and photos in your report.

Moving from best practices into actual research and measurements

In this chapter we have studied the many perspectives on bias and best practices through all the phases of a research project involving children. We are now ready to put it all to use in actual studies. The following two chapters will firstly look at how actual measurements, the scores, in a study cannot be confused with *recommending an experience to others*. Then, secondly, I will demonstrate how the measurements can serve as a helpful tool for understanding not just the experience of one group of children but also how experiences may differ and can be compared across perspectives such as gender, age, culture, and time.

Toward Infinity and Beyond: A KX Score

In this chapter firstly we will look closer at different types of research with children and the types of data we can obtain from them and better understand what we can realistically expect from user research with children. It will show that adult cognitive abilities, specifically their meta-cognitive abilities and their abilities in math, separate them (well, us) both as researchers and as respondents from children. We cannot rely on self-reporting to the same extent as with adults and this behooves us to focus on different research methods than on those we would use if adults were our respondents.

Through user research with children we need to reliably measure children's experience in order to develop new and better products and services in the future. We need to study one experience in itself, but also in comparison with other experiences (is it better or worse? – why?). We actually have a long list of research needs in that we need to compare the experience of younger children with that of older, the experience of children in one culture with that of children in other cultures, and also we need to compare how the experience of the same children changes over time (e.g., as they grow and acquire new skills, but also as their context changes, for instance, with the arrival of new technology). We need a universal scoring system, a score.

© Thomas Visby Snitker 2021
T. V. Snitker, *User Research with Kids*, https://doi.org/10.1007/978-1-4842-7071-4_4

Some will argue that we already have such a score, in the shape of the Net Promoter Score (NPS), so this chapter will, secondly, take a long hard look at what the NPS is and how it works when it comes to research with children, because – when it comes to inspiring decision-makers, innovators and, designers with actual meaningful facts – it doesn't work well at all. However, the NPS remains a force to be reckoned with. In many companies the bottom line and the Net Promoter Score are the guiding lights when it comes to running the company. So as a researcher you are very likely to come across it. This chapter, however, will argue that researchers (and companies) that rely mainly on the NPS, whether its score is based upon children or their parents or both, run the risk of looking at irrelevant numbers and making uninformed decisions.

Some of the things we can (and can't) learn from children through research

In Chapter 1 we saw that a big factor in research with children are actually the children's adults (e.g., teachers or parents) and the view on children's role in society. In Chapter 2 we took the painstakingly long journey through the many potential biases in research with children. Chapter 3 highlighted the regulatory requirements. In this section we will study some of the methodological limitations and opportunities because we *do* have a broad and deep arsenal of tried and true research methods at our disposal.

Here are the main research avenues:

Through interviews (usually semi-structured interviews) we can ask for example "*What do you think of this toy?*" and get an open-ended verbal response. Instead of asking for a verbal reply, we can ask for a drawing or a diary post as a written reply.

Through questionnaires we can ask, for example, "*Do you like this toy?*" (notice the Yes/No scale) or "*How much do you like this toy?*" (notice how it lends itself to a degree or a scale, for instance, to a large degree) and we will get a closed-form verbal response. Instead of a verbal reply we can ask for a written response.

We can use observational techniques and ask children to "*Go about your day as you normally would.*" This would give us open-ended behavioral or performance data. If instead we ask them to solve a specific problem or task, we would get closed-form behavioral or performance data.

Ideally we will combine these methods and build upon their individual strengths. If, for instance, we were to study an existing product or service or if we were to come up with ideas for new products, we could start by observing open-ended behavior, then ask open-ended questions, and lastly build a questionnaire to see how widespread a given behavior or sentiment is. We might want to focus on the children's replies only or supplement with the caregivers' replies. We might also include data from the surroundings and other contextual sources in the study.

There are several challenges though. As an adult researcher, it can be tricky to understand precisely the differences in the replies we can get from fellow adults as opposed to those we can get from children, but it is clear that in most cases adults have more cognitive resources available as respondents (e.g., in how we solve tasks, respond to problems and challenges, and how we make choices by actively encoding, processing, and recalling needed information) than children do, for example:

- Adults can better reflect on their own behavior.

- Adults can better reflect on their own reflection.

- Adults can more accurately compare their own desires and behaviors with those of others.

- Adults can better articulate themselves generally and specifically about their own reflections.

- Adults are more tolerant of a research situation – they understand which role they are expected to play in a research situation and they can play it better.

The tricky part is that the cognitive activities of self-reflecting, comparing, articulating, and having situational awareness are so integral and automatic to most adult reasoning and being that adults give little thought to these processes themselves. So adult researchers risk being unaware that these cognitive factors need to be recognized and taken into account to a much larger extent in research with children. One example is numbers and math, which we will look closer at in the next section.

We can count how many children go through a process

The secret language of statistics, so appealing in a fact-minded culture, is employed to sensationalize, inflate, confuse, and oversimplify. Statistical methods and statistical terms are necessary in reporting the mass data of social and economic trends, business conditions, "opinion" polls, the census. But without writers who use the words with honesty and understanding and readers who know what they mean, the result can only be semantic nonsense.[1]

—Darrell Huff

To many people – the CEOs of many companies, for instance – the NPS is a very meaningful number. Other meaningful numbers relate to the marketing and sales funnel (or, in ecommerce, the conversion funnel), which in these days include a host of channels[2] both in respect to adult and child audiences:

- Owned channels such as your website, our channel on YouTube, or our page on Facebook (where the age limitation is 13 years, so not likely to be an intersection with children), our publications, etc.

- Earned media where our customers talk favorably about our products or services via messages on social media platforms such as TikTok or Instagram (but not likely with children as the age limitation for both services is 13 years), or through word of mouth

- Paid media, such as advertising on our channels (and again: most likely on YouTube), in search results, or on TV or outdoor media

To marketeers it is meaningful to understand this as a funnel, where in each step you aim to optimize the number of children who proceed to the next step:

- How many children were exposed to and
- ... actually paid attention to the media (or advertisement)
- How many children liked it
- How many understood it
- How many considered it
- How many reacted to it
- How many responded to it
- How many desired it
- How many children asked their parents to buy something based upon it

---

[1] https://en.wikipedia.org/wiki/Darrell_Huff and How to Lie with Statistics (1954)
[2] https://en.wikipedia.org/wiki/Earned_media

- How many had a positive experience when consuming it
- How many children were inclined to recommend it (e.g., an NPS) and potentially
- … ask their parents to buy it again

It also makes sense to look at this process from a transactional perspective, the conversion from seeing something to desiring something to doing something, without any monetary elements. Children are unable to make as many actual purchases as adults, but often the tactics remain the same – someone (e.g., marketeers, publishers, broadcasters, or producers) try to lead people through the funnel to a desired outcome whether it is to make a purchase or to ask some else to make it for you (e.g., which a child could do through a wish list). Attention economics[3] considers a child's attention (as well as that of an adult) as the scarce resource that it is, and "converting someone" through the process outlined here requires a lot of attention on the part of the "converted." In this sense, the child has paid for a video on YouTube with the currency of their attention, which, as it turned out, was not spent on any of the millions of other ways to spend one's attention on, say, YouTube.

In reality the funnel is actually a sieve as children inherently will leak out from step to step in bigger or smaller numbers except for those rare cases where everyone who saw the ad, reacted to it, and bought the product (in which case I speculate that the number of kids is relatively low, making the word funnel a bit grandiose – perhaps a straw is a more appropriate metaphor).

We need to be careful with numbers in user research with children

Here are some examples of the opportunities and pitfalls related to using numbers and arithmetic as part of research with children, for example, as something we ask of children in test tasks or evaluations. It is a very familiar territory for adult respondents, but not navigable for children until perhaps age 7–9.

Following a sequence of numbers in order to draw a shape (such as in Figure 4-1) is a simple task – but only when you have learned the sequence of numbers (i.e., learned how to count!).

---

[3]https://en.wikipedia.org/wiki/Attention_economy

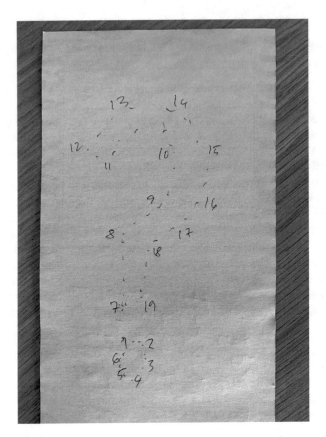

Figure 4-1. Connect the numbers – it may not be as easy as adults think

Arithmetic is another example of what most adults would consider trivial cognitive tasks that nonetheless require learning. You, dear reader, would likely not need much time to complete the following tasks:

This...	...equals:
10 + 20	?
30 + 40	?
50 + 60	?
70 + 80	?

You probably very quickly added the numbers together. But let's take a step into the pre-math brain of a 6-year-old by looking at the following results:

This...	...equals:
10 + 20	2
30 + 40	2
50 + 60	3
70 + 80	4

How can this be true? See the explanation in the footnote below.[4] Besides their numerical values, the numbers have a geometric significance that is so apparent that a 6-year-old will see it (and count it, but not perform the arithmetic), whereas your post-math adult brain simply can't help but perform the task it has been taught to do. We ignore the obvious, even though the "numbers" are right in front of our eyes. The post-math brain cannot easily be turned off. This can lead us to include numbers and math in our research, which can be misleading if we put children in front of them. If, for example, one needs to expand a study originally designed with adult respondents in mind to also include children, one cannot simply repeat or reproduce the research approach. Let's take a closer look at the NPS, a very widely accepted method and one that is an example of a research method originally designed for adults but also applied to children, since it sits in the intersection between business, research with children, and quantitative methods.

We can ask children if they would recommend something to a friend – or not

Evangelistic customer loyalty is clearly one of the most important drivers of growth. While it doesn't guarantee growth, in general profitable growth can't be achieved without it.

—Fred Reichheld[5]

---

[4] You don't add but count the number of circles in each equation.
[5] http://hbr.org/2003/12/the-one-number-you-need-to-grow/ar/1 http://hbr.org/2003/12/the-one-number-you-need-to-grow/ar/1. The NPS metric was first developed in 1993 by Fred Reichheld and later adopted in 2003 by Bain & Company (where Reichheld had been working since 1977) and Satmetrix as a way to predict customer purchase and referral behavior.

The NPS works by asking a question uniformly across all the possible touch points with the customer: "*How likely are you to recommend this product to a friend, on a scale from 0 (not likely) to 10 (very likely)?*" The responses are calculated and averages produced:

- A score below 7 is interpreted as a "detractor," someone who devalues your product.

- Only 9 and 10 are categorized as "promoters."

- 7 and 8 are called "passives," "indicating that they are not likely to actively recommend your company to others" (I find this to be a questionable term, since it describes people whose answers were in the middle of the two other positions, but who are hardly passive in any sense).

It can be assumed that the responses given by adult and child cohorts of detractors may differ in their level of dissatisfaction, and specifically the adults can be characterized as follows, if we view it from the perspective of the company evaluating its NPS:

- Those who are very unhappy and have already decided to discard our product and now they want to tell us why

- Those who are frustrated and actively researching and considering alternatives, but haven't decided to abandon us yet

- Those who are disappointed by certain aspects of our product or a single interaction, but they still think our product or service has potential and want to help us improve it

- Those who are unhappy and only use our product out of necessity and aren't actively considering switching to an alternative, but want to voice their complaints and criticism

But what about the children, can they be grouped in a similar fashion? Can they in fact be considered to have the same cognitive resources available to provide a credible rating as adults have? This is one of the first concerns we should occupy ourselves with. To deliver meaningful and reliable insights to our stakeholders, we need a measure of the children's experience that builds upon their own cognitive abilities, whatever they are.

The question of "*How likely are you to recommend …?*" is not about how happy customers are with the product or service, but rather around how likely they are to recommend the company in general, or the service or product specifically. A company can use the calculated score to indicate its potential for real, sustainable growth through customer retention and word-of-mouth referrals.

The point of the NPS is to try to connect the survey responses (specifically: ratings) from actual shoppers to a behavior (recommending something to someone) that is meaningful in a business context. The NPS is currently not being challenged on the marketplace as a most meaningful number, but there are, of course, many alternatives from other market researchers. The main question is if the number allows you to learn something of business value, and in this context if it is a useful way to conduct research with children. Let's go through each step of the process to see.

"How likely would you be..."

There is a philosophical problem in extracting "something" of business value (e.g., knowing if people will buy your product in the future) based upon people's answers to a post-shopping survey about whether they would recommend the product to others.

One bias in the survey itself is that there is no accountability for the respondent: no one will check if the respondent (should the occasion to recommend arise) actually did recommend the product to anyone. Or if the respondent had 10, or 100, opportunities to recommend the product to someone, and the average of these actual recommendations corresponds to the statistics (is equal to the imagined recommendations). In addition it's anyone's guess if respondents will answer truthfully or not about their own likely future recommendation activity.

"... to recommend <insert product name here>..."

Another bias is due to putting people in the hypothetical situation of *recommending*. Consider all the products you, as an adult, buy in a month – groceries, consumer goods, services. Looking at your bank statement will give an indication of the number of transactions, but will not say if you bought 5 or 10 items in each transaction. I would venture to guess that most adults buy at least 100 different products or services a month. Perhaps many, many more. Children aged 6–10 years, on the other hand, buy much fewer, perhaps less than 20 products a month. Where one challenge to adults *recommending* is that they purchase so many products, the opposite seems to be the case for children; the suggested weekly allowance in the United States in 2019 from one source[6] is 50 cents to a dollar for each year of a child's life, so a monthly income for a 7-year-old of $14–$28.

But how likely are adults and children to *recommend* products or services to a friend? Think of ten products you buy regularly. How likely are you to recommend those ten products? It seems like a strange question – unless, of course, it is a natural part of your behavior. Do you go around recommending products? Or are you on the receiving end of recommendations from your friends all the time? Do you even *want* frequent shopping advice from your friends? Or is it acceptable only in certain cases – perhaps you have an unspoken understanding between you and your friends with regard to which items or product categories are okay to discuss and which are a "no-go"? Perhaps you'd say, "Yes, let's share sneaker recommendations, but no, let's not share toothpaste recommendations"?

The act of recommending in general (so not just products or services they've purchased but also activities they enjoyed or places they went, etc.) provides social currency to the recommender, and is clearly a normal part of human interaction. But compared to all the other topics of conversations among friends, for example, "how are you?", "where are you?", "do you want to hang out?", "when and where?", "do you want to go out?", etc., the act of recommending products is probably fairly uncommon in most people's lives. Until the conversation finally touches upon a product – let's say sneakers – and you talk about the sneakers you've just bought and that's *maybe* interesting to your friends because they care about you. But the actual NPS score you give is, of course, only relevant to the friend who is currently in a sneaker-shopping mindset. The problem is, because of the way the NPS is constructed, it pretends that a behavior that occurs naturally, but rarely, among friends (i.e., recommending) can be generalized and scaled through recommendations among hundreds and thousands of strangers, and then work just as well as a score.

"… to a friend?"

The point of this chapter is to highlight and discuss those areas of children's life or experiences that are suitable for research and specifically if the NPS is suitable. Friendships sound like one of them, so let's dive into this area.

The underlying premise of the NPS is that it is easy or natural for a respondent to imagine recommending something to a friend – that as a respondent you likely don't reject the NPS question. Instead, you probably imagine an actual friend or someone who's like you, then you imagine them in the same context as you, and then use them as a proxy for your answer.

---

[6]www.babycenter.com/child/parenting-strategies/giving-kids-an-allowance-what-you-need-to-know_10304079 quoting Kristan Leatherman, the coauthor of *Millionaire Babies or Bankrupt Brats? Love and Logic Solutions to Teaching Kids about Money*

So would it be fairer to address the other part of the question: *a friend?* Maybe the NPS score will make more sense if seen through the relationship, the friendship, rather than through the experience of the product or service? My first thought is that the friendship angle is a methodological distraction from the main intention of the NPS: the experience for the respondent (not the friend) is what may potentially inform the product's stakeholders, since the respondent (adult or child) cannot speak for the friend's experience with any level of precision. But let's give the friendship angle a closer look.

According to the Oxford Dictionary,[7] a friend is "a person with whom one has a bond of mutual affection, typically one exclusive of sexual or family relations." Let's take a closer look at friendships. Especially adult friendships are well documented, but unfortunately those among kids are not.

A Gallup study[8] found that, in 2004, on average adult Americans have almost nine "close friends" (a mean of 8.6), not including their relatives. 45% of Americans say they have six or more close friends, 39% have between three or five close friends, and 14% have one or two close friends. Only 2% of Americans say they have no close friends.

Adults with children under 18 have slightly fewer friends (an average of 7.3 friends vs. 9.4 for those with no children).

The poll shows that one's age matters as, on average, those aged 65 and older have an average of 13 close friends, compared with an average of 9 friends for those aged 18 to 29 and 50 to 64 and 7 friends for 30- to 49-year-olds.

To sum up: quantitatively, the pool of friends that adult NPS respondents can pick from is likely small, and I will assume that the size of the friends pool is roughly equally small for children.

The *qualitative* characteristic of friendships of NPS respondents is less transparent – does any kind of friendship qualify, any *depth* of friendship? Is a close friend more welcome to give or receive recommendations? I would argue that the closer the friendship, for adults and children alike, the better we know the friend's wants and needs, and this allows us to give better recommendations to closer friends. The act of giving recommendations is in some ways similar to giving gifts: it is a sign of interest, commitment, care, and a desire to increase the bonds of friendship. It can be seen as a way to impress or reward a friend and to add value to a relationship.

---

[7]www.lexico.com/en/definition/friend
[8]https://news.gallup.com/poll/10891/americans-satisfied-number-friends-closeness-friendships.aspx

But, on the other hand, the relevance of the recommendation must reflect the domain of the friendship. For instance, the recommendations can clearly not include any areas of contention between the friends, or areas that the friends keep secret from each other.

In addition to this, there are other qualities and nuances that can make friendships unstable reference points for recommendations, namely

- Friendships can be temporary and vaguely defined. You may consider someone to be your friend who, in their mind, does not consider – or no longer considers – you a friend. Since childhood is marked by growth and exploration, I will speculate that this is even more common among children than adults.

- Some friendships are limited to certain domains or activities, such as a football friend, a friend on social media or even a pen pal (which is probably an unknown term to most contemporary children). Some friendships are limited to certain seasons, such as those you only see at work or school, or those you go out or on holidays with.

Are all these different types of friends relevant to the NPS question? Since the term friend is not defined as a part of the NPS question, to me it raises the concern that we cannot assume that all NPS respondents share the same definition of friendship. When it comes to friendships and children, research in psychology through the years has firmly established that friendships, and in particular reciprocated friendships, are important for children's self-worth and peer identification in middle childhood.[9] In 2019, British psychologists Rachel Maunder and Claire P. Monks studied 314 children between the ages of 7 and 11 and concluded that

having reciprocated friendships can buffer against a poor quality best friendship in relation to a child's feelings of self-worth, and friendship quality mediates the relationship between having a reciprocated best friend and identification with peers.

This quality of friendships is far more interesting than the aspect of recommending a product. To be reliable and relevant as a score and as a business metric, the NPS needs to span a broader range of qualitative and quantitative characteristics of friendship than it currently does.

---

[9]"Friendships in middle childhood: Links to peer and school identification, and general self-worth" published in British Journal of Developmental Psychology (2019), 37, available here: https://onlinelibrary.wiley.com/doi/full/10.1111/bjdp.12268

"… to a relative?"

Perhaps instead of recommending to a friend, we might consider recommending to a relative.

The pool is certainly larger than the pool of friends. A French study of nearly 2000 respondents in 1990[10] counted ascendants (parents, grandparents, great-grandparents), descendants (children, grandchildren, great-grandchildren), and collateral relatives (siblings), and found that (and we can assume that this is true for both children and adults)

- An individual's immediate family circle (including the family-in-law if there is a spouse) includes 15 immediate relatives on average.

- Adding a similar number of uncles and aunts, nephews and nieces (non-immediate relatives), the average family network totals around 30 people.

- Partners in a conjugal union necessarily have a larger family (18 immediate and 23 non-immediate relatives on average) than persons living alone (10 immediate and 16 non-immediate relatives).

- Couples report being emotionally close to around five people in their family, while singles are close to three.

When comparing the number of (close) friends – around nine on average – to the number of (immediate) relatives – approximately 15 on average – it is clear that the pool of relatives is larger. Maybe there's also a little bit of an overlap: your sibling, parent, or child may be one of your friends. And increasingly so, according to a study from 2016 by Google Ipsos Connect.[11] It found that 8 out of 10 millennial parents in the United States agree that their child is one of their best friends.

But comparing the quality of the relationships one can have with these two groups, it is also clear that friendships in most cases are shorter with friends than with relatives. However one's friends are likely to be closer in age and interests than one's relatives – perhaps with the exception of one's cousins, siblings, and siblings-in-law.

This – as we are thinking about friends and relations – seems like a good place to mention the apparent lack of context in the NPS question. Fact: I bought this product for myself just now. NPS question: Would I recommend others do the same? Concern: Well, yes, if they had the same needs, the same criteria

---

[10]www.ined.fr/fichier/s_rubrique/264/relatives.en.pdf
[11]www.thinkwithgoogle.com/data/millennial-parenting-statistics/

for buying (e.g., preferences), and the same funds available as I did. But how do I know if that is the case? They would have to be very similar to me – and also find themselves in a context similar to mine, so the question requires the respondent to take a large leap of faith (or specifically: a large leap of context).

In this chapter we are looking for relevant indicators or dimensions for research with children and, specifically, if recommendations are relevant. With respect to the NPS, then, we can conclude that relationships with relatives are perhaps more relevant to *recommendations* – certainly quantitatively (people have 1.5 times as many relatives as friends) but also somewhat qualitatively (people have longer relationships with relatives, though age and interest tend to be more similar between friends).

As an aside, to understand the theoretical upper limit on the number of friendships, we can turn to Dunbar's number. British anthropologist Robin Dunbar found that humans can comfortably maintain 150 stable relationships (actually 148, but he thought 150 would be a nice, round number).[12] But this is an aside. Let us proceed to another aspect that is potentially relevant to research with children – if we can use a scale and if so, which scale?

... scored on what scale?

A fourth bias comes from the relationship between the individual numbers in the score (0–10) and the experience the respondent had. The Net Promoter Score is calculated based on responses to a single question:

> How likely would you be to recommend
>
> <insert company/product/service here>
>
> to a friend or colleague?

The scoring system for this answer is based on a scale from 0 (not likely) to 10 (very likely). Clearly 4 is less than 5, but what does that difference mean to the respondent – what words or concepts does the respondent associate with the experience that would translate to a 4 or a 5?

To take a different approach, if one is to ask how old the respondent is, or what product the respondent is most interested in, the answer is likely very

---

[12] 150 would be the group size only for communities with a very high incentive to remain together. For a group this large to remain cohesive, Dunbar speculated that as much as 42% of the group's time would have to be devoted to social grooming. Thus, only groups under intense survival pressure, such as subsistence villages, nomadic tribes, and military groupings, have achieved the 150-member mark. Dunbar noted that such groups are almost always physically close, which means that modern-day online friendships don't count toward Dunbar's number. Robin Dunbar (1992): "Neocortex size as a constraint on group size in primates." *Journal of Human Evolution*

easy for a respondent (child or adult) to interpret. Their age is a fact, and the most interesting product is named directly. The problem with using a scale like the NPS lies in determining what it actually refers to: if there exists a direct relationship between the score and a word or concept in the world. Or – if there is no direct relationship – what construct, trait, or concept underlies the respondent's score on a measure (so-called construct validity[13]). In short; there is not an agreed-upon experience or concept that uniquely scores 4 (or 5, or any other number) on the NPS – neither for individuals nor for society as a whole, neither for children nor adults. Differentiating between 4 and 5 (and likely other numbers) is arbitrary – the same respondent might not know the difference, might not have experienced the difference in any conclusive or universal manner. There is no yardstick or even words to differentiate between 4 and 5 – as opposed to referring to numbers in the real world (4 or 5 cakes is very meaningful if you are 4 or 5 people) or to established concepts (like math; 4 in itself is less than 5).

Even assigning a score of 0 or 10 may not be commonly agreed upon, as cultural norms differ greatly over the globe and likely also across consumer segments. If we presume that one culture is more inherently skeptical and another is more inherently trusting or naive, as does Geert Hofstede in his concept of uncertainty avoidance,[14] one can assume that, in assigning a score, the sceptic and the naive will interpret the question ("How likely are you...") differently. If you try sounding out the question in a skeptical voice and then in a naive voice, you can almost hear the bias.

One of the advantages of the NPS is its indexical nature – that in asking the same question over and over again it keeps the inherent bias the same over time, allowing us to track fluctuations in the respondents' sentiments over time and over different sources. As a consumer of NPS (e.g., a researcher or decision-maker), it is important not to be trapped by the natural appeal that an index offers: that it appears to reflect a measurable reality, that it is a fact, like the temperature, or (to remain in a business context) how much a product has sold. There is no natural default setting of an NPS score. Clearly a lower score is worse and a higher is better, but there is no definitive threshold for a good or bad score. An index may well make you think as much, but this is just the brain playing tricks on you. The strength of the NPS is not that it measures something (i.e., customer satisfaction) correctly, but that it measures what it measures in the same way every time. As its proponents will point out, whatever bias exists in the measurement is constant.

Therefore, the actual value of the NPS is in the variations that may show up over time, in its upward and downward fluctuations, and that it allows its

---

[13]See "Scale development: ten main limitations and recommendations to improve future research practices," Fabiane F. R. Morgado, 2017: https://link.springer.com/article/10.1186/s41155-016-0057-1
[14]https://en.wikipedia.org/wiki/Hofstede%27s_cultural_dimensions_theory

users to analyze and hypothesize about the reasons for these changes, and to redesign their offering in order to optimize their score.

Another advantage is that the NPS – as a side product from the quantitative findings – can also harvest other useful types of feedback, such as comments that can be analyzed. A drawback in this regard is that most people – and specifically children due to the fact that one needs to provide textual input – are reluctant to give accurate and elaborate responses in a survey (a self-administered questionnaire, to be exact) that has a question like "Please elaborate on why you gave this score?" and a nice big, blank text input field. Most likely you will find that people keep their open responses short in surveys, so much so, in fact, that all the nuances that would normally exist in a face-to-face or phone interview disappear. Also, since the subgroup of respondents who answer the open questions are self-selecting and the response rate is lower than it is for other, nonoptional questions, open answers are ultimately a very unreliable source – likely filled out only by the happiest and least happy customers. As a result, the open answers are likely to paint a completely different picture than what the numbers themselves depict. Another obvious drawback is that the survey will only capture those experiences and thoughts that people are willing and able to verbalize (or, textualize) and that can accommodate the time and energy available to the respondents at that particular moment. Asking a Why question invites complex cognitive reasoning. It may be a very good question but consider other, less demanding, ways of asking it.

Choosing which scale to use in research with adults and even more in research with children is a bigger question than it may appear at first glance, which is a topic that we will also revisit in the Chapter 5. A ten-point scale (such as the NPS) may seem like a natural choice – we do have ten fingers and toes (most of us) and the decimal system is used widely in society. However, in many other areas where we wish to gauge the weight or intensity of the respondent's preference, a Likert scale,[15] named after the American social psychologist Rensis Likert who came up with it in his PhD in 1932,[16] of five or seven points has proven very efficient. This is because it deals with many of the biases mentioned in Chapter 3 but also other biases that are pivotal to quantitative studies, such as *central tendency* bias (in which respondents favor a response in the middle out of a desire to avoid being perceived as having extremist views). For some reason the Likert scale was disregarded for the NPS.

---

[15]https://en.wikipedia.org/wiki/Likert_scale
[16]https://en.wikipedia.org/wiki/Rensis_Likert

... why?

But there is something missing here. As you manage and develop a company or are involved in its design, innovation, and business development, you clearly need to understand your brand's health and financial situation. However, neither figure will tell you if your customers understand your products, if they are able to make the most out of them, or if they use them as intended. In other words, these two figures will not tell you if your products are delivering good experiences to your customers.

From a management, innovation, design, and development perspective, you can have the best financial reporting and excellent NPS scores, but if you have little or no visibility into the performance or quality of the experiences you produce, you will not know whether you are doing well or poorly. You will not know if you should carry on as is or stop and make changes. The financials will tell you which products sold well, which sold poorly (and so on), and the NPS will tell how this has impacted your brand. But unfortunately, neither will tell you why.

Nor will they tell you if it is likely that consumers will abandon your product the moment a new and better experience comes to the market. For example, non-smart mobile phones were extremely popular and probably had great NPS scores right until smartphones came to the market. Altavista and Yahoo were the top search engines until Google was launched.[17] This very day we – adults and children alike – are using products that we find awesome, but which will be obsolete and perceived as intolerably dated in the near future. Can NPS scores help us with this? Can they help us determine what *good* is?

The NPS is not a KX score

To sum up, the NPS has shortcomings in several areas:

- There's no accountability for the respondent, whether it is an adult or a child.

- The situation of recommending is hypothetical.

- The friendship angle is a methodological distraction from the main intention of the NPS: the respondent cannot speak for the friend's experience with any level of precision.

---

[17]Here's a trip down memory lane: www.makeuseof.com/tag/7-search-engines-that-rocked-before-google-even-existed/

- Quantitatively, the pool of friends that NPS respondents can choose from is likely small.

- Friendships are so full of nuances that they make them unstable reference points for recommendations.

  As an aside, relationships with *relatives* are perhaps more relevant to recommendations, certainly quantitatively, but also somewhat qualitatively.

- There is a lack of context for the recommendation

- The scale in itself: There exists no direct relationship between the score and a word or concept in the world.

- Most people are reluctant to give accurate and elaborate responses in self-administered questionnaires anyway.

- The NPS cannot help us understand *why* a product is scored as it is.

- It can't tell us what is good or if a product has staying power — developments in the market may well have made it superfluous tomorrow.

This leads me to conclude that in general the business value of the NPS is low, because it provides a false narrative about the value of the brand or product, and specifically in research with children it does not provide any solid platform for decision-making. This chapter took the NPS as a starting point for an exploration of the areas of relevance for research with children, realizing that it is limited how much we can learn only through qualitative research (which depends upon our ability to hear what children say and to inspire them to give feedback) or only from quantitative research (which again depends upon us giving children adequate and precise ways to give feedback).

The aspiration of the NPS is to predict the future behavior or preference of shoppers or those who influence the shopper, but the NPS figures can be misleading (or perhaps I just take them too seriously). It may be in place to offer a concerned and skeptical view toward the perceived *trust in numbers* (which I will reference again in Chapter 6): Once you can put a number, a percentage, to an experience, the number *becomes* the message, becomes the truth or insight, rather than what's behind the number. It's not that I disapprove of numbers, quantitative studies as a whole, or "data" (whether "big data" or small) — in fact, I believe that a company *needs* to run on numbers. But it is *because* of this need that the numbers must be credible, must be based on something that is actually quantifiable in a meaningful way, that should not count, more or less, random children's opinions out of context or record their fleeting attitudes.

On a more general level, we must be aware not to blur the lines between social science (which examines the relationships between individuals and societies – such as how many people understand a message, why they opt to travel through the sales funnel, and give a favorable review of that experience) and natural science (which studies the physical world, including the laws of biology and math).

My objection is that numbers and scores can give a false impression of impartiality and universality, and that they can suggest irrefutable facts that appear to be set in stone. Numbers can misleadingly portray an ambiguous, dynamic world with precise, unambiguous figures. Well, the problem is not with the numbers themselves, but in the way that they are valued and used by people, both individually and in society and commerce.

Arguably a more relevant figure when you are designing and producing customer experiences is a *customer experience* score rather than a net promoter score. If you have never heard of such a score, fret not, as there is no well-established concept for this nor for any collectively agreed-upon standard for calculating such a score. Not yet, at least. In Chapter 5, I would like to propose constructing and implementing just such a score, well, a *kids'* experience score.

What to Score

There is definitely the need for a score that would allow everyone involved in the design and innovation process to understand how a product or service is *really* experienced by its intended audience.

The score would indicate if there are major differences between the experiences of different audience segments. For example, it would tell us if 6–8-year-old boys enjoy it more than 9–11-year-old girls, if the same age and gender group in two different cultures have different experiences, or if the same service across different tech platforms perform differently (e.g., if a game works better on a smartphone than on a computer).

The score will allow us to compare the experience against similar and/or competing services and products, and also compare different versions of the same product. The score is *horizontal* in that it can encompass every type of product or service that we can see, and *vertical* in its measurement of real people's experiences. A pretty tall order.

The System Usability Scale, SUS

The inspiration for this score came from the *System Usability Scale* (SUS). Originally created by John Brooke in 1986,[1] it allows researchers to evaluate a wide variety of products and services, including hardware, software, mobile devices, websites, and applications. The SUS consists of a 10-item questionnaire

---

[1] In 2013, an interesting retrospective by John Brooke himself was published by the UXPA, here: https://uxpajournal.org/sus-a-retrospective/

© Thomas Visby Snitker 2021
T. V. Snitker, *User Research with Kids*, https://doi.org/10.1007/978-1-4842-7071-4_5

with five response options for respondents: from Strongly agree (1) to Strongly disagree (5).

For example, the first four statements are:

1. I think that I would like to use this system frequently.

2. I found the system unnecessarily complex.

3. I thought the system was easy to use.

4. I think that I would need the support of a technical person to be able to use this system.

By asking the same set of questions to users across all kinds of products and services ("systems") in a uniform way, we can obtain a uniform basis for comparison.

But we cannot ask these kinds of questions to kids: it's all too abstract and "meta" (reflective and self-reflective), even if you change the wording. Children are often not trained in reflecting upon their experiences, let alone in answering questions about them. Some children are not comfortable answering questions from strangers with great detail and precision, even if their parents are sitting next to them.

Another source of inspiration is the *Child Self-Reported Playfulness* (CSRP) *scale* by psychologists Elian Fink, Silvana Mareva, and Jenny L. Gibson from the University of Cambridge.[2] It is part of an undertaking to develop and test the psychometric properties of a self-reported playfulness metric for kids in the 5–7 age range. The authors discuss how play literature has so far been dominated by teacher and parent observations of, and reporting on, children's play (both solitary and social peer play). They argue that young children's own voices and perceptions of their play and playfulness tends to be overlooked.

The authors derived the following statements from other research sources and presented them to a total of more than 300 children by means of two puppets in a video. The puppets each described themselves using one of two bipolar statements, presented with a neutral intonation, and the child was asked to point to the puppet that was most like them. Also their teachers were interviewed in order to compare the self-assessment with an external measurement.

---

[2]The study is described in the chapter "Dispositional playfulness in young children: A cross-sectional and longitudinal examination of the psychometric properties of a new child self-reported playfulness scale and associations with social behaviour" in the book *Infant and Child Development*, published by John Wiley & Sons Ltd (2020). It can be found here: https://onlinelibrary.wiley.com/doi/epdf/10.1002/icd.2181

1. I do not really look for fun things to do

   I often look for fun things to do

2. I make up new games to play

   I do not make up new games to play

3. I do not sing and dance very much

   I sing and dance a lot

4. Other kids think I'm fun

   Other kids do not really think I'm fun

5. I do not tell funny stories

   I tell funny stories

6. When someone else starts something fun, sometimes I do not join in

   When someone else starts something fun, I always join in

7. When I have to do something boring, it's never fun

   When I have to do something boring, I try to find a way to make it fun

8. I tell jokes

   I do not tell jokes

9. I always follow the rules

   I do not always follow the rules

10. I always play pretend

    I do not really play pretend

11. I do not often do silly things so other people will laugh

    I do silly things so other people will laugh

Playfulness and the quality of being fun and lively can clearly be relevant parts of a child's experience, so the CSRP score is meaningful in and of itself. However, the study's process and methodology are also inspiring in the context of measuring children's experiences.

Another source of inspiration was the *Consensual Assessment Technique* (CAT), put forward by psychologist Teresa M. Amabile of the Brandeis University,[3] which deals with the social psychology of creativity and how to test for creativity.

In early 2021, around the time this book was being finished, a group of researchers at B&O, Preely, and Aalborg University (Lars Bo Larsen, Tina Øvad, Kashmiri Stec, Lucca Julie Nellemann, and Jedrzej Czapla) published their case study *Development of a framework for UX KPIs in Industry*.[4] It aims to assess and track the UX quality of products (for adults), in order to ensure that the desired level of quality is met, to clarify potential areas of improvement, and to compare competitor products via benchmarking. They are also inspired by well-known UX scales such as the UEQ and AttrakDiff, as well as more business-oriented measures, such as the NPS score discussed earlier in this book and the CES score.

A KX – Kids' Experience – score

The purpose of the score is to assist the broadest possible range of our stakeholders – both laterally and vertically, and inside our organization as well as with externals. Therefore, the score's target audience includes designers, product owners, project managers, developers, support staff, decision-makers – pretty much everyone with an interest in the users' actual experience of a product or service.

When to produce the score?

It is possible to extrapolate the score beginning around the time in the development phase when there exists a workable prototype that can simulate the intended user experience, and continuing from then on into the launch and post-launch phases and subsequent iterations. In fact, the whole point of the score is to measure it more than once, preferably every time a major improvement in the product or service is available to test.

Actual major improvement or "major improvement" – the quotation marks are added to emphasize that it is an unsubstantiated claim made by a team that clearly intends, thinks, and hopes that the changes are also actual improvements but they have not actually studied it. In fact, the score will be

---

[3]*Journal of Personality and Social Psychology*, 1982, Vol. 43, No. 5, 997-1013, https://prod-uct.design.umn.edu/courses/pdes2701/documents/5701papers/01creativity/amabile82.pdf

[4]https://vbn.aau.dk/en/publications/udvikling-af-bruger-oplevelses-kpier-for-industribrug-et-case-stu, (the paper is in English though the URL is in Danish) published by OzCHI 2020: 32nd Australian Conference on Human-Computer Interaction (HCI)

the highest authority on whether the new version is indeed an improvement or simply... well... a new version.

Another occasion for running the score is if new user segments are added. This may be the case, for instance, if the product has recently been launched in a different part of the world, or if the context of the product or service changes radically – for example, if a new competing product with groundbreaking new features comes onto the market, or if the marketing campaign changes profoundly. Another occasion might be if the pricing structure or distribution model changes, and if these changes are significant to the user experience. In practice, the occasion to run the score again may simply be the existence of available bandwidth on the project team or among the researchers. This implies that the actual measuring of the score must be *planned* in order for it to get done. It implies that when you plan to produce the first score, you should also plan roughly when to produce the next one.

Who does the scoring?

When we developed a kids score, our first decision was to play to the strengths of research with children rather than to the weaknesses (as described in the section on SUS earlier). Instead of letting the child self-analyze their experiences, the actual scoring needs to be done by an adult: either the moderator (live or subsequently) or a notetaker or observer. This allows us to keep the points of research interest instead of dumbing down the study itself by reducing its complexity or scope. Instead of the moderator asking questions and the study using the answers as the primary focus point, the moderator encourages behavior, which then becomes the primary focus point. The quality and amount of talk during the session is irrelevant, and a conversation may happen more fluidly or freely, based on the energy of the situation.

Score what exactly?

In order for the score to be relevant in the design and innovation context, we developed the following criteria:

- The score must enable comparisons of experiences across all relevant audiences and touch points

- The score must encompass all types of interactive media regardless of device or platform, for example, web, app, game, or building instruction on iOS, Android, or PlayStation

- The score must include all genders, cultures, and ages

A literature review turned up little of relevance, but we found the following sources helpful:

- *Measuring the User Experience* by Tom Tullis and Bill Albert (2013)
- *Quantifying the User Experience* by Jeff Sauro and James R. Lewis (2016)

These books helped us to understand the requirements for a quantitative study when it comes to a minimum sample size and suggested that we define the scope of the Kids' Experience score in terms of the number of respondents to at least 30 per homogeneous segment – for example, one gender and one narrow age interval (e.g., 8–9-year-olds) from one culture. This means that we would need 60 kids in order to study the same material in the same age and gender group but over two cultures.

We also used the literature to help us find a suitable number of research dimensions. The list of areas of interest could quickly grow and become hard to manage. We ended up with five main dimensions, each consisting of between 10 and 20 indicators. The five dimensions remain constant across all studies, but the indicators may vary from project to project depending on their relevance to the study. For example, in the dimension Familiarity, which relates to how well known the concept and content is to the respondent, if the purpose is to study a given app the indicators will be other comparable apps where in a study of a game the indicators will be other comparable games. Let's have a look at each of our five dimensions.

Engagement and curiosity

This dimension deals with the extent to which the app, game, website, or other kind of system engages the kids and creates a desire in them to learn more.

The indicators include

- Do the children seem interested and engaged in the system?
- Do they go back and repeat something that they enjoyed?
- Are they curious and inquisitive, for example, by exploring all the functionalities or areas of the system?
- Would they like to know more about any characters or plots in the system?
- Do they spend more time than actually needed, because they are engaged and curious (the so-called time spent)?

Usability

The main focus in this dimension is on the usability of the functionalities: if the kids are able to do what they want or need to do at a suitable pace, to navigate to where they want to go, and to begin and end the use of the product or service (system) in a suitable manner.

The indicators are classic usability parameters, such as

- Is it clear to the children where in the app or game they are at any given time, and how they may move on or return to the beginning?

- Do the kids err or hesitate?

- Do they waste a lot of time trying to figure out how the app or game works? (this time wasted should be correlated with the time spent being curious, as noted earlier)

- Do they understand metaphors and iconography, texts, colors, and illustrations? (Recall the notions about text readability and respondent age in Step 9 "...using the right device" in Chapter 2.)

- Do they fail or succeed at performing a task? And if they fail, do they figure out how to recover and proceed?

If it is a game, do the children quickly figure out the objective, the mechanics, and the controls, or not? If there is a scoring system in the game, do they understand how it works and what they need to do to win?

Familiarity – conceptual and content

This dimension is usually the hardest to explain. The point of the dimension is to learn whether the kids are able to build upon any existing knowledge from past experiences in order to help them understand what the app, game, or system is. The opposite would be that the experience is completely foreign to them and that they need to learn everything about it – its genre, concept, and content elements.

With regard to this dimension, researchers need to recognize, on the one hand, that there is a first time for everything and that this novelty is part of the thrill or intrigue of an experience, while, on the other hand, a design with familiar elements will be easier to understand and use. Researchers should understand that both of these aspects can coexist in a system, and, in fact, this is a sign of good design. The dimension of familiarity seeks to discover if the overall universe of the system makes sense to the children.

The indicators include

- Do the children understand or grasp what genre, class, or category the system is, for example, which stylistic traits or modes of function can belong to this category?

- For example, in one app we had an avatar – an icon or figure representing a particular person – and by including this in the Familiarity dimension we could study if this is understood by the children, or if, in contrast, they find it confusing.

- If there are characters (e.g., cartoon figures) in the system, do the children recognize these characters and know what they stand for (their personalities, so to speak)? Do the kids find that the characters act according to their expectations?

- If the system features a plot and any kind of world or universe, does this make sense to the children? Does the system use artifacts or conventions that the kids find are well suited and relevant to that plot or world?

Awareness and salience

In this dimension we study to which degree the kids notice the elements that the designers intended the kids to notice. Salience (from the Latin *salire*, meaning "to leap") describes something that leaps out at you because it is unique or special in some way. This includes if the children notice everything from the name of the system, to the options that they have at any given point, to any prominent visual features or significant messages throughout the system.

The indicators should be derived from the priorities that the designers and developers have – it may, for instance, be the intention of one system that the kids clearly notice all the navigational elements, whereas in another system the designers may have intended for the navigation to be as subtle as possible.

Satisfaction and fun

This dimension is not as closely linked to the fact that the system is supposed to be fun as it may seem at first glance. As any adult knows, a system can be satisfying to use without being fun. Take an ATM, for instance. When it dispenses the expected amount of cash, you are satisfied, but likely the process wasn't a lot of fun in itself. Not all systems designed for kids intend to be fun, but often it is relevant to study the extent to which children have fun using it, as this dimension will influence the mood or expectations they will have with regard to using the system, and most likely also the output or experience they will glean from it.

This is closely related to the first dimension, Engagement and curiosity. Systems that are fun and satisfying are likely also engaging and inspire curiosity – and vice versa. However, the two dimensions are still relevant on their own: having fun is, in its own right, a central quality to any children's activity, and it is important for designers to understand if this, in fact, occurs in their system. In addition to this, kids can potentially have plenty of fun in just one part of a larger system, which could reduce their curiosity and interest in exploring the rest of the system. In which case both scores are highly relevant.

The indicators can be observational (are the kids smiling, laughing, signing, attentive, etc.?), but in this particular dimension we can also choose to rely on two types of feedback from the children. One is a satisfaction questionnaire designed particularly for kids and based on a 5-point Likert scale but with smiley symbols instead (going from a very frowny face to a very happy face). The other is verbal feedback from the children: we ask them if they liked the experience ("did you have fun?") but we will leave it up to the moderator or notetaker to vet whether the response fits the behavior they observed. If the moderator observed a child clearly having fun, that is what should be scored, regardless of what the child said afterward.

Other evaluation criteria are relevant

These five dimensions are not the be-all and end-all of evaluation criteria. Inspiration can be found in many different places. If you'd like to study how children experience a product or service with learning in mind, the LEGO Foundation's *Learning through Play* tool[5] offers a holistic approach to learning that comprises the full breadth of skills, including cognitive, social, emotional, creative, and physical.

In building the tool, the LEGO Foundation and partners have examined the body of literature on learning through play and concluded that play is educational when it is *joyful, meaningful, actively engaging, iterative, and socially interactive*. Each of these five dimensions lend themselves to measurement in an experience or learning score and can serve as a framework.

---

[5]The white paper "Learning through play at school," by Rachel Parker and Bo Stjerne Thomsen (2019) is here: www.legofoundation.com/en/learn-how/knowledge-base/learning-through-play-at-school/

In the white paper, the five dimensions are broken down into *five states of play*: from passive, to exploring, owning, recognizing, and transferring. Again, these could also serve as parts in a score, either on their own or together with the five dimensions.

How You Can Use the Kids' Experience (KX) Score

Chapter 5 described what the KX score is and how we developed it. This chapter is more hands on. It will go through the process of setting up a score (e.g., what goes into a score) and I will discuss various ways of applying it (e.g., which scales to use). The intention is to equip the reader with a solid platform for introducing a KX score tailored to the reader's own context and to focus the attention on the most challenging parts of that journey.

KX score setup – an example

Imagine a scenario where you need to understand how kids aged 8–11 find ideas for their Christmas wish list on major web portals such as Amazon, Wish.com, and eBay. Which portal does a better job at helping the children? The KX score can determine this in a transparent way.

© Thomas Visby Snitker 2021
T. V. Snitker, *User Research with Kids*, https://doi.org/10.1007/978-1-4842-7071-4_6

Here's a way to break down the five dimensions into practical test tasks and observation points.

Step one: Determine what success is

This step aims to determine what describes a good experience for children that are looking online for ideas for their Christmas wish list. It's easy to sum-up a bad experience; they can't find anything and get confused and frustrated in the process. The result of a good experience on the other hand is that they found relevant products and enjoyed the process, so now we'll break that into measurable chunks, using the five dimensions I introduced in Chapter 5 as parts of a KX score:

- Curiosity: Do the children pick the first thing they look at (lower score) or continue exploring (higher score)?`

- Usability: Are they able to navigate through the pages, to search, to understand the content (higher score) or not so much (lower score)?

- Familiarity: Do they understand what the website, the categories, and the products are about, and are the terms familiar to them (higher score) or confusing (lower score)?

- Salience: Do they notice all the pertinent information, such as price, shipping time, if a desired product is in stock or not (higher score) or do they not notice it (lower score)?

- Satisfaction: Are they happy with their experience from the beginning to the end of their visit (higher score) or are they frustrated, hesitant, doubtful, or unable to find relevant information or products (lower score)?

Step two: Determine what sort of user behavior is indicative of success or failure

Here are some examples:

Curiosity

1. Looks at more than 3 pages

2. Looks at more than 2 categories

3. Uses internal search machine

Usability

1. Navigates without hesitation
2. Navigates without errors
3. Can save product (wish) for later

Familiarity

1. Recognizes individual products
2. Recognizes product groups
3. Recognizes product categories
4. Recognizes site brand name
5. Recognizes site branding elements (logo, colors…)

Salience

1. Notices key product details
2. Notices product pricing
3. Notices if in stock or not
4. Notices if it ships and if it arrives in time for Christmas

Satisfaction

1. Says that it was a good experience or not
2. Found that the products were displayed well ("pretty" or "easy to see") or not
3. Would use this site again another time

Here is an example of how the process might look in practice.

Aligning the KX score with business goals in practice

During the scoping and preparation phases of a study, we meet with the designers and developers to agree on what the study should include and how we will run it.

It may be that the purpose or scope of the study is not suitable for a score – for example, if the time and resources we have available don't allow us to run 30 sessions per homogeneous subsegment. Or the project may explicitly need qualitative, but not quantitative, input.

To establish which indicators to use, we collect all possible inputs ("what would we like to learn here?"), for instance, in a workshop, and then we categorize them according to the five dimensions. We aim to have 5 to 10 indicators per dimension. Fewer indicators would mean that the individual indicator will have a high weight in the overall score, which is undesirable unless that particular indicator is uniquely interesting to the study. More indicators will risk stressing the data collection and clutter the analysis phase with less important details.

Once the indicators have been solicited and organized into the dimensions, we can build a note sheet. The sheet will leave each individual indicator open for a score from 1 (low/worst/not) to 5 (high/best/highly). Using a five-point score (as opposed to a 10-point or 7-point scale), allows multiple notetakers to score more in alignment with each other, but the higher alignment will come at the risk of potentially reaching a lower level of detail and precision. But the simpler the scale, the more able we will be to clearly articulate why we assign a particular score.

"Beauty is in the eye of the beholder," a proverb goes, meaning that beauty doesn't exist on its own but is created by observers. To avoid this also being the case if you put a group of trained researchers in front of (a video recording of) a user research session (in which the score is in the eye of the annotator), the process of scoring can be harmonized and aligned through training and discussion. For instance, have the observers watch the same video sequence and assign scores on an individual basis, then reconvene and discuss. If there are outliers in the scores, discuss them and agree on a guideline for scoring. This may sound easy but it's not, especially if you have a team with varying levels of practical research experience, or if your project is marred by vague purposes (e.g., if the purpose is to learn "Is it a good experience?" without having defined indicators of "good").

In a seminal study[1] of how well (or poorly, as it turned out) researchers are aligned in their designations of the severity of a usability problem (if it is a cosmetic, minor, major, or severe problem), usability expert Rolf Molich[2] conducted a study to investigate whether inspection results (so not scores from actual user research sessions, but close enough) from independently conducted professional inspections differed as much as usability test results. It turned out that they did.

---

[1] www.dialogdesign.dk/cue-3/
[2] Rolf Molich has a long and glorious career in usability. With Jakob Nielsen (already quoted in Chapter 2) he developed the most-used usability heuristics (guidelines, or rules-of-thumb) for user interface design back in 1990. In 2014, the User Experience Professionals Association awarded Rolf the UXPA Lifetime Achievement Award in recognition of his work on the Comparative Usability Evaluation studies (CUE) and heuristic evaluation.

The results were staggering due to *the evaluator effect* – that different evaluations (or evaluators) point to considerably different revisions (or scores) of the system they evaluate.[3] In this study 11 usability specialists individually inspected a website and then met in four groups to combine their findings into group outputs. Although the overlap in reported problems between any two evaluators averaged only 9%, the 11 evaluators felt that they were largely in agreement. The evaluators perceived their disparate observations as multiple sources of evidence in support of the same issues, not as disagreements. Thus, the group work increased the evaluators' confidence in their individual inspections, rather than alerted them to the evaluator effect:[4]

> The evaluator effect would be less critical if severe problems were reported more consistently than cosmetic problems, which have little impact on a website's usability. A problem was defined as severe if it appeared in one or more executive summaries. Each evaluator reported an average of 24% of the 33 severe problems. Seventeen (52%) of the severe problems were reported by just one or two evaluators. Hence, the evaluator effect persisted for severe problems.
>
> The substantial differences in the individual reports stand in stark contrast to the perception the evaluators acquired during the group work. They left the group work with a strong, and reassuring, feeling of agreement. This became evident during the plenary session, as exemplified by the following quotes from five of the evaluators:
>
> - "I was surprised to see how little we disagreed."
> - "A very high level of agreement."
> - "It is not that subjective after all. There is consensus about what the problems are."
> - "General agreement, but a number of concrete details differ."
> - "We are all in agreement. We haven't made the same observations, though."

---

[3]Here's a thorough break down of numbers: https://measuringu.com/evaluator-effect/
[4]www.dialogdesign.dk/tekster/cue3/cue3_paper.pdf

Nobody countered these statements.[5]

Having multiple moderators (or evaluators or annotators) will help reduce the evaluator effect but only if they agree on what is what. So one must make sure to set aside time for moderators to align their scoring framework before they start observing the children's behavior. Once annotators are well aligned, each session will only require one annotator.

The scores can be defined as either task related or experience related. For instance, see the following tables:

Scoring task performance

Score	Label	Pass or Fail	Description
5	Easy	Pass	1st try – no problem
4	Medium	Pass	2nd/3rd try – observed difficulty
3	Hard	Pass	3rd/4th try – expressed difficulty
2	Assist	Fail	Succeeded with assistance
1	Fail	Fail	Failed or gave up

This scale clearly requires moderators to be very observant of tries and to be deliberate when assisting, to give any assistance only in very measured amounts and to take note of their assists.

Scoring experiences

Score	Label	Description
5	Fantastic	Very fun, very engaging, and very relevant
4	Great	Fun, engaging, and relevant
3	OK	Mostly fun, mostly engaging, and mostly relevant
2	Bad	Mostly boring, mostly confusing, and mostly irrelevant
1	Horrible	Boring, confusing, and irrelevant

The scores should be set only on the indicators and not set on an entire dimension, as the dimension score in itself is an abstraction since it sums up all of the child's behaviors and experiences in that session – the indicators

---

[5]Morten Hertzum, Niels Ebbe Jacobsen, and Rolf Molich, "Usability Inspections by Groups of Specialists: Perceived Agreement in Spite of Disparate Observations," CHI2002 Extended Abstracts, ACM Press, pp. 662-663, www.acm.org – see www.dialogdesign. dk/tekster/cue3/cue3_paper.pdf

have a more specific and direct relationship with that behavior or experience than a dimension score will have.

Then, after the 30+ sessions, we will calculate the average score per dimension across all sessions, and we'll calculate the average across all five dimensions. A score of 3 can be medium but we cannot know if it is good, adequate or bad in itself. We can know if it is better, the same, or worse if we compare it with the scores from a similar test with different children or with a different system. Or, alternatively, if we compare it with a new test of a revised version of the same system with similar kids at a later point in time.

We can expect to find a few beneficial side effects of introducing a kids' experience score.

Firstly, it encourages prototype design that focuses on the kids' experience. In the dialogue with the designers when scoping and preparing the study, we found that anchoring the conversation in the kids' intended behaviors (rather than the design per se) helped to focus the test materials (e.g., the prototype) on the most central value-add of the product or service: what would be on the kids' agenda rather than what was on the designers' and developers' agenda. That way, by simply having a score, it forces the designers to interpret their design intentions into intended behavior.

Secondly, it creates a shared language that focuses on the kids' experience. The terms from the score creep into the designers' and developers' language and become a part of our shared vocabulary. This in itself makes it easier for designers to focus and to optimize their work toward the benefit of the end audience.

Finally, it builds momentum. Having scores from previous months and quarters makes the organization aware of future research needs and prompts managers and key stakeholders to follow up on the scores by carrying out new, updated studies.

Build your own experience score

The hardest part of having a tailored experience score is not building it, but implementing it and sustaining it through continuous, rigorous research activities.

However, once you have it going, it gathers momentum and will institutionalize the focus on the user experience.

Build behavioral indicators

If you wish to build your own score based on this framework, the main task is to build dimensions and indicators that directly correspond to those user or customer behaviors that are central to your business and that generate revenue.

If, for instance, a main focus is on the acquisition of new customers, dimensions should include how and when new customers become aware of your offerings, and how and when they convert from browsers to shoppers. Indicators should include how well they understand product descriptions, if they are able to differentiate between and compare various products, and how easy it is for them to go through a sales funnel.

Define audience (sub)segments

Another task is to define the audience, and preferably the main subsegments. You can consider using *frequency of task* or *past domain experience* as key differentiators (both concepts were introduced in Chapter 2 in the description of respondents), as these are often very relevant to understanding how subsegments perform and why.

In the case of the Kids' Experience score, age is a way to condense past experience, when it comes to both domain experience (how familiar they are with a given phenomenon, e.g., playing an online game) and physical abilities and motor skills. But once your audience is grown up, age, in most cases, becomes meaningless as a definition.

The experience score has a twist when it comes to certain product domains – specifically, those products that come with manuals, for example, washing machines, routers, exercise equipment, medicine, or musical instruments. The twist is that the manuals (or sheet music) are there to advise and encourage correct usage. The scoring system for these types of experiences will inherently lend itself closely to the instructions for use, and the system will likely score the adherence to these instructions. However, the results and scores will nevertheless still be highly relevant to the companies that produce those washers, routers, or pianos, and sheet music, as they will allow them to study how well their audience or user groups perform with and perceive their products as well as the competition's. In addition to this, a score will allow the companies to not limit themselves to survey answers based on the likelihood of promoting the product to a friend.

If you consider three different levels of experience with your product or service – for example, novice, intermediate, and super user, as described in the section "Skill level as a descriptor" in Chapter 2 –, you have a good starting point for an initial segmentation for your experience score, and thus which three groups of users to include in your ongoing study, whether the users are children or not. This may appear counterintuitive if you think along the lines of market segmentation, where your primary focus will be on those market clusters with the largest potential – that is to say, those clusters with the largest population. If, for instance, you are in "new tech," super users will likely not be your primary focus, as the tech is *too* new for anyone to have acquired sufficient experience to become a super user.

In the perspective of the Experience Score (as opposed to that of conventional market research), even a small segment can be relevant, as the results from the niche segment, when compared with the scores from other segments, will provide a much more nuanced score.

Thinking of your subsegments in the terms of frequency of task or past domain experience can also offer an alternative to simply using demographics such as gender, income, geography, or the like. Demographics may be relevant in a market perspective but less so in the context of the audience's experience.

Collate and test

Ideally at this point in the process you have

- Something for the kids to interact with (the stimulus)
- A list of behaviors that each indicate an intended experience
- A description of your intended audience

The behavioral indicators need to be in a sequence similar to that of the user's intended journey through the experience, in the form of a journey map, task list, or similar. This list and the accompanying score (1 to 5) can be the template for a moderator or notetaker's sheet that can be used during the research sessions (in each just replace the X with the appropriate activity or feature that is specific to your product).

In table form it will look something like Figure 6-1.

	Respondent 1	Respondent .....
Dimension 1: Engaged and curious 1.1 How engaged in X are they	*	*
1.2 To what extent do they explore X	*	*
.... (up to 1.9)	*	*
Dimension 2: Usability 2.1 To what extent are they able to do X	*	*
2.2 To what extent are they able to do X	*	*
... (up to 2.9)	*	*
Dimension 3: Familiarity 3.1 To what extent do they understand X	*	*
3.2 To what extent do they understand X	*	*
... (up to 3.9)	*	*
Dimension 4: Awareness 4.1 To what extent do they notice X	*	*
4.2 To what extent do they notice X	*	*
... (up to 4.9)	*	*
Dimension 5: Fun 5.1 To what extent do they enjoy X	*	*
5.2 To what extent do they enjoy X	*	*
... (up to 5.9)	*	*

Figure 6-1. This is the moderator's or notetaker's scoring sheet

*Score from 1(worst) to 5 (best)

With your scoring sheet ready, you then go through the usual preparation steps (e.g., pilot testing and recruiting), and then the testing begins. The less the moderator interacts with the child during the scoring-related parts of the session (the sheet), the more precise the scoring. The session can include other parts, such as a pre-test interview to ensure that the recruitment was correct and to learn about respondents' background and past experience, and a post-interview about their experience in the session. It will be during the post-interview that the moderator can ask the child to retrospectively add more details to their experience and allow the moderator to correct or update the scores assigned during the test.

Score and report

As an example, the sheet might look like Figure 6-2 after three sessions with respondents a, b, and c:

Name, gender, age	a	b	c
Curiosity and			
Are they curious about	3	3	3
Are they curious to	3	3	3
Do they get to the	4	4	4
Do they get to the	4	4	4
Do they get to the Sets	3	3	3
Do they get to the Apps	3	3	3
Do they go back and	4	4	4
Do they want to explore	1	1	1
Usability			
Do they know how to	3	3	3
Do they understand the	3	3	3
Do they notice and use	3	3	3
Do they notice and use	4	4	4
Do they understand the	4	4	4
Do they understand the	2	2	2
Are they able to upload	2	2	2
Are they able to build an	2	2	2
Do they log in?	1	1	1
Familiarity			
Do they understand the	1	1	1
Are they familiar with	4	4	4
Are they familiar with	3	3	3
Salience and awareness			
Do they notice all of the	3	3	3
Do they notice all of the	3	3	3
Do they notice the	3	3	3
Do they notice the	3	3	3
Do they notice the	3	3	3
Do they notice the links	3	3	3
Satisfaction			
Did they find the app fun	3	3	3
Would they recommend	3	3	3
Were they excited about	3	3	3
Did they like the overall	3	3	3

Figure 6-2. Score sheet after three sessions

These detailed scores can then be aggregated into final scores, which give the average across each indicator (e.g., 1.1) and each dimension (e.g., 1.1 to 1.9), as well as all a total score (Figure 6-3).

	Score
Curiosity and engagement	
Are they curious	3,0
Are they curious	3,0
Do they get to the	3,7
Do they get to the	3,7
Do they get to the	3,0
Do they get to the	3,0
Do they go back	4,0
Do they want to	1,0
Usability	
Do they know how	3,0
Do they	3,0
Do they notice	3,0
Do they notice	4,0
Do they	4,0
Do they	2,0
Are they able to	2,0
Are they able to	2,0
Do they log in?	1,0
Familiarity	
Do they	1,0
Are they familiar	4,0
Are they familiar	3,0
Salience and	
Do they notice all	3,0
Do they notice all	3,0
Do they notice the	4,0
Do they notice the	3,3
Do they notice the	3,6
Do they notice the	3,0
Satisfaction	
Did they find the	3,0
Would they	3,0
Were they excited	3,0
Did they like the	3,0

Figure 6-3. Aggregated final scores across all dimensions

This would lead this study to produce the score shown in Figure 6-4.

	Score
Curiosity and engagement	2,7
Usability	3,4
Familiarity	1,8
Salience and	4,3
Satisfaction	4,1

Figure 6-4. Scores for the five dimensions

This is not especially helpful in itself, but if you repeat it over time it will produce a trend, as in this example in Figure 6-5 of a product that improved over time in all dimensions.

	Score January	Score March	Score May
Curiosity and	2,7	2,8	3,1
Usability	3,4	3,5	3,9
Familiarity	1,8	1,8	2,1
Salience and	4,3	4,4	4,9
Satisfaction	4,1	4,2	4,7
Total	3,0	3,0	3,4

Figure 6-5. Scores for the five dimensions at three different times

And if you had subsegments of respondents aged 6, 8, and 10 (each consisting of at least 30 respondents), then you can be more specific and study if and how the experience score differs amongst the age groups (Figure 6-6).

	Score 6-yo's	Score 8-yo's	Score 10-yo's
Curiosity and	2,7	2,8	3,1
Usability	3,4	3,5	3,9
Familiarity	1,8	1,8	2,1
Salience and	4,3	4,4	4,9
Satisfaction	4,1	4,2	4,7
Total	2,7	2,8	3,1

Figure 6-6. Scores for the five dimensions and three different age groups

This can be continued and combined ad libitum as long as it's meaningful. Perhaps you'd like to report how the product scores in different cultures, or across genders. Perhaps you'd like to compare how this product scores against a different product with the same audience, or how it compares to a previous version of the same product, or against its prime competitors.

The versatility of the score (the broad approach to experience testing) is its strength – it allows you to compare different *relevant* people *actually experiencing* a product across virtually any parameter, as opposed to, say, the NPS, which allows you to compare how likely people in a survey are to recommend something to their friends.

Here, at the end of the chapter on the KX score, and right before you hopefully start including this in your research arsenal, it may be useful to remind ourselves of a general caveat to scoring or quantification, to *trust in numbers*.[6] The purpose of the score is to compare reactions and behaviors in different individuals (e.g., across age, gender, culture, or whatever) to the same stimulus (a product or a service, such as an app or website) and to learn if the product or service resonates differently with different audiences. The score also allows us to compare how different but comparable stimuli (e.g., a previous and a current version of the same product, or a competing product) is used and appreciated by an audience. Just keep in mind that the point of the score is to *supplement* – not to *replace* – qualitative research.

---

[6]*Trust in Numbers* is the title of the book by Theodore M. Porter (Princeton Paperbacks 2016; www.amazon.com/Trust-Numbers-Theodore-M-Porter/dp/0691029083) that examines the role of quantification in science and research.

Challenges and Opportunities in Research with Children as Seen by Practitioners

Research always happens in a context. This book has focused on challenges I have met and lessons I have learned. To broaden the horizon of the book I'd like to share contexts and perspectives from formidable seasoned research professionals in a variety of practice fields, so I interviewed a small but diverse group consisting of

© Thomas Visby Snitker 2021
T. V. Snitker, *User Research with Kids*, https://doi.org/10.1007/978-1-4842-7071-4_7

- Researchers working purely in a commercial context as well as some who work in philanthropy and in close collaboration with academia, policymakers, and administrators.

- Researchers who work as consultants on different projects "all the time," as well as those who work on one single product.

- Researchers who work solely as researchers and some who also have other roles, such as producer.

- Researchers who work with a broad range of respondent groups and contexts, as well as others who focus mainly on one: for instance, school teachers and the classroom, or the child on their own in their time off.

- Researchers who generally have a global focus and those who need to adapt to different specific local cultures.

- Researchers with digital experiences as their only area of work and researchers whose work spans other areas as well.

- Researchers who focused specifically on the research profession through their studies and their career, and those who've worked in related fields such as quality assurance, design, marketing, and innovation.

Perhaps this variety will inspire you to see a broader context for research and for the research profession!

Learning and research through play

Garrett James Jaeger is Research Specialist in the LEGO Foundation. I have mentioned it a few times earlier in the book, but to recap it is the nonprofit organization that brings together academics and practitioners in child development and creativity with the aim of building a future in which *Learning through Play*, a central mantra in the LEGO Foundation, empowers children to become creative, engaged, lifelong learners.

Here are some examples of their many projects:

- The development of an affordable, high-quality, play-based early learning network for children aged 0 to 5 in Nairobi, Kenya.[1]

---

[1] www.legofoundation.com/en/what-we-do/programmes-and-projects/affordable-play-based-early-learning-network-kidogo/

- The "Play Prescriptions" project aims to encourage caregivers to play with their children at home, currently in Latin America.[2]

- Two projects in Mexico use robotics to promote learning through play in informal learning environments. In one, children aged 6–9 learn about teamwork, science, and technology. During a 14-week program, they work in teams, research a topic, create scenarios, and learn how to build and program a robot. In another project, robotics workshops have been organized for youth centers across the state to allow for adolescents, who visit these after-school centers, to benefit from the playful learning experiences.[3]

The practical implementation of a project can include a variety of deliverables, such as

- Product donations, for example, Play Boxes and Learning-through-Play activity booklets

- Training: Development of a "Training of Trainers" model, including a group of 25 Master Trainers and over 300 trainers throughout the country

- Supervision: Supervision visits to ensure quality

- Play Standard: A competency standard to ensure that any practitioner in the country can be certified as a Learning-through-Play facilitator

- Curriculum: Development of a new curriculum ensuring that play is prominent throughout the program

- Advocacy: Influencing other service providers, both public and private, on the importance of Learning through Play

Garrett's projects thus look at the places where play and learning intersect. The input for projects comes through a large network of academics and policymakers, the actual projects involve many and diverse stakeholders, and the output intends to create actual change for children around the world. Research with children in this context needs to consider practical implementation in schools around the world (it needs to be "teacher friendly") and must be politically relevant in the local cultures, while at the same time incorporating the scientific rigor that I describe throughout this book. Garrett

---

[2]www.legofoundation.com/en/what-we-do/programmes-and-projects/play-prescriptions/
[3]www.legofoundation.com/en/what-we-do/programmes-and-projects/robotics-programme-mexico/

works on establishing metrics that can monitor and develop the implementation of the projects, ensuring that children have a good experience in a way that does not burden the teachers or the administrative system around them.

The role of the researcher in this type of research is to make sure things are pragmatic but also useful from a metrics standpoint. Garrett highlights that there is rigor to ensure that a study will show enough variance and an effort that allows him and his colleagues to ask better and better questions going forward. Some of the challenges revolve around diversity, ecological validity, and the age grouping of children, specifically the following.

How can we increase cultural diversity and ecological validity?

One question that comes up in his projects is: To which extent can we make generalizations based upon studies coming mainly from one culture, for example, from the United States? Garrett says

> Many times our research is from that WEIRD[4] sample: the white privileged communities, middle income and such. At the LEGO Foundation we really push to see how well we can confidently say this would work in Ukraine as well as it would in Mexico City or in South Africa or Kenya. So that comes up a lot for us.
>
> When I look at the regions covered by the LEGO Foundation, I am struck by how internationally diverse their efforts are, so the answer to the question (can they increase diversity?) is yes – and simply put, the best way is to actually have a strategy of diversity and follow up in each individual project in the scoping phase by including different cultures as much as possible.
>
> Does our research have ecological validity, or in other words, does what we're looking for *actually* have meaning, and does it *actually* align with what we do?
>
> Yes, we want researchers to come in and produce great research, but we also need to be implementation researchers so that this evidence will work for us in

---

[4]WEIRD is an acronym for samples that are drawn from populations that are White, Educated, Industrialized, Rich, and Democratic. Ninety-nine percent of all published studies rely on participants recruited from populations that fit those criteria, according to this source: www.psychologytoday.com/intl/blog/thinking-about-kids/201710/attracting-weird-samples

the field and also be very pragmatic for those who do the study and or use the evidence so that it's very meaningful. That's a really big question.

One of the aspects of this question, which we will now focus on, revolves around the age groups included.

How do we group children by age?

This theme has come up several times in this book, and for Garrett's work it adds an extra dimension in that the stakeholders change significantly with the different age groups.

It makes a tremendous difference if we talk about children aged zero to three, or three to six and six to nine. Not only does that mean a lot of difference in what we're looking at, but it also means that we're working with different stakeholders. So what if we're going three to six? Who's in that conversation, and how do we link in their information? Those are some very fundamental child development questions, but there's also some very fundamental policy and pragmatic questions.

Garrett points to a central dilemma in research with children:

Even though as a part of the science and our training we try to put kids in categories so that we can measure things from a research perspective, they're still crazy diverse. The diversity of children is amazing, even though we're trying to put them in categories. The reward is that we'll never be done with this and that the questions keep coming. And they get better and sometimes they get worse but I think the diversity of children's behavior is amazing.

Can children accurately tell us about their thinking and experiences?

One of the challenges relates to the children's limited ability to self-report or have metacognition on what they did or what they're thinking.

This can be up to six years old, sometimes eight, could be even nine. The assumption that they're going to accurately tell us what they're thinking is a really big assumption, and that's a really big challenge to assume that we're getting decent data when there they vary so much on what they are aware of and their own thinking.

Garrett points to one of the ways to address this:

This is why it's really important to have process analysis that allows us to see what unfolds as it happens because if we're only looking at the output we're missing all of these other things that maybe the child doesn't know how to describe. Maybe we don't need them to tell us, if we can pair up what they're telling us with what we're observing in measurements to see if it is reliable.

The intersection of policy questions, research rigor, and cultural context

The policy questions involve what kind of communities are involved in those decisions.

If we are going into a community or cultural context, we want to co-create, that's our ambition. The policy question is *"who do we need to have in the room in order for that to happen?"* It almost always starts or ends with the Minister of Education or some connection there to make sure that if we're going to be doing this research that it's something that's useful for them, because if we can't get in the room to make a change with these evidence, then we're just contributing to a body of literature, which isn't a bad thing, but we're moving into very much an implementation research approach, and so it's not about just contributing to the literature and the subject.

Working with policy makers, administrators or even employees can challenge the rigor of the research if they demand a result that is too simple or too streamlined. [Jennifer Wells will echo this idea later in the chapter.]

Sometimes they want that silver bullet, they want that really top headline piece. And it's not always that clean.

Garrett is very aware of the need for rigorous research and the need to avoid things that are not tested as rigorously as they should be. Still, he points to the fact that if the study is only going to end up in journals or in textbooks, it may only impact a handful of researchers.

> I can have all the scientific rigor in the world, but if it's not something we can scale up or roll out, there's a tradeoff there. We try to lobby for as much rigor as possible, but also have to have a balance – is this practical? And is this something that we can actually do, and that requires a lot of people making compromises and us developing and adapting as well?

> It is important to understand that this is a BOTH/ AND conversation, such that one way is not better than the other. There is a role for experimental psychologists who investigate a very specific process of how curiosity impacts learning outcomes, and that those findings need to find a way to be applicable in the classroom for them to increase value beyond a peer-reviewed journal. While research certainly pushes our understanding along to progress and provide further clarity, classrooms are much messier than a laboratory experiment, and we seek out research findings that can translate well into effective classroom applications.

Impact through getting the right people together around the right insight

In order to succeed, many things need to fall into place, and this requires a very broad perspective on the project and the stakeholders involved.

> Our perspective is holistic in the sense that we are responsible scientists and making sure that we're respecting everybody, and that there's a system.

In the system, Garrett and his colleagues' insights are part of a process that uses protocols and procedures on processes to ensure they are collecting evidence aligned with GDPR. The work includes database management and knowledge management as well as procedures on how to share the information.

> Some of our research we want to share and so it's not just the researchers or the evidence team that gets to look at those evidence. It's how do we make it meaningful for people who are rolling out our programs in Kenya? We don't always speak the same language. And so we have a lot of translation work to say, *hey, what is the best way for you to understand this?*

> without, you know, talking down to people. And at
> the same time we need to understand what's going on
> in the field so that we're not just in our ivory tower
> asking, really, you know, highfalutin questions.

This echoes many of the considerations in the latter part of Chapter 2 – for instance, Step 16 (A simple and focused presentation) and Step 17 (Sustaining the findings).

In order for his research to be useful, Garrett works to get people from the evidence team into initiatives with people who are working on programming or policy and advocacy so that people are in the same room.

> That is a start. I think there's a facilitation that needs
> to happen that we start speaking similar languages. It's
> very challenging and at the same time very rewarding.

Plan for surprises, and use pilots!

The range in which children can stay engaged with the study, or the range in which their behaviors can vary, brings challenges and surprises every time. Even when we have the best plans for a research study, we're inevitably surprised at how much more information is available. And sometimes it doesn't align with the questions that we want answered. Garrett points to a general challenge to research with children:

> Often the measures that we use aren't flexible enough
> or don't have a broad enough range. If we don't pilot
> enough, if we rush in based on just going off of
> literature, we're definitely going to be surprised, and I
> think that's something as a researcher of children that
> you can't put enough stress on: preparing through
> piloting, preparing through not only the literature
> being sound but that you go through and test to make
> sure that you're doing what you set out to do.

To Garrett, what makes research with children challenging is also what makes it rewarding.

> It's children, I mean it's full of surprises. From a
> research perspective you can adapt to it, but I think
> that one of the biggest best things about working with
> children is that it is a surprise. All the time. Like wow,
> they really are amazing learners and they are able to
> teach us things not only by how we're observing but
> how we interact with them. And it's in many ways
> when the biggest surprise are challenges,

As researchers we are supposed to stay in a script, be rigorous and be aware of the way that we administer a variable or a factor, the way that we administer some sort of input or prompt, but there's many times we're like, oh, I can't believe they just did that and it's hard to be disciplined in that way.'

Are we measuring? Or having illusions?

Confirmation bias (also mentioned in Step 12 in Chapter 2) comes up in Garrett's work as a huge problem, and to him it has practical as well as philosophical implications.

Something you always have to be aware of is: are you getting what you're looking for? Before I became a scientist, I went to a Buddhist University and learned that the word Maya which is prominent in a lot of Eastern traditions literally translates to measurement. But it also means illusion. I think it's really important for us to understand that we can use measurement as a tool, but it's also illusory. It can always change, and you're always going to miss something. Like the saying: when you're a hammer, everything looks like a nail. I think it's really important for us to make sure that we are flexible and diverse in the way that we measure things.

Science is only one of many ways that children learn

Scientists tend to frame learning as science, and that's a problem if it means that children can only learn by using experimental methods and scientific methods to evaluate. Garrett highlights that there are many ways in which children can learn, and it's not just scientifically.

Science explains a lot and it's amazing, but there are many other perspectives and paradigms from which we can view how children behave and learn. Play is one. It doesn't have to be just testing a hypothesis. They may not even generate a hypothesis. They may just be interacting with something and they don't have to be conscious of it either. Also introspection – where children are just thinking about something, or visually testing things, imagining things, it doesn't have to be a science.

This book is about research rather than learning, but the way Garrett describes this problem points to a clear parallel between learning and research with children: on the one hand we need to rest firmly on science when we conduct research, but on the other we miss out on a broad range of children's experiences if we only rely on scientific rigor.

You continually learn from children, both as a researcher and as a person

Garrett talks about how children's learning abilities (both how much and how well they learn) are a perpetual well of inspiration and motivation.

> They are the best learning organisms that we know of, and it's inspiring and they can teach us! Even though we as adults have more experience doesn't mean that there's not something we can learn. Not just from the study, but also just from us being around children.

He points to how what children experience in learning through play at a young age still ripples or echoes through what we as a adults try to do when we are learning how to become a parent, when we're learning how to do our jobs better, when we're trying to be a better friend, or when we're trying to navigate projects at home or at work. Garrett ties up how learning and research and a career as a researcher go hand in hand in this way:

> I think our learning as a child is still there as adults and we can learn from children. And I think that is a huge reward and it's still relevant for me as a human and I think that's amazing.

Producing digital experiences and researching with children

Jennifer Wells is a thought leader in children's digital experiences. She has launched over 60 digital products and managed concept and business development for major international brands, including LEGO (where I first met her), PBS KIDS, Universal Studios, The Jim Henson Company and many others. "I've kind of gone from pure entertainment to pure education and the whole spectrum in between," Jennifer explains.

Steve Jobs featured one of Jennifer's first apps, SUPER WHY,[5] during the initial launch presentation of the iPad, and the first suite of PBS KIDS apps were downloaded over 6 million times in three years.[6]

While there are many career paths that can lead to user experience research with children, they often go through design, communication, or engineering. But Jennifer's path is unusual:

> I've been a producer for many years but my focus as a producer has always been the user experience so I'm probably a bit unusual in that regard because I'm not so much about the facts and figures of the production as I am about making sure that what we're producing is the right experience for the kids that we're trying to reach.

Currently she is a director of production for California-based Code Spark Academy (Figure 7-1). Their product is designed to help kids learn coding skills through gaming, under the motto "Preparing kids everywhere with the skills they'll need for the world of tomorrow."[7]

---

[5]www.pbs.org/parents/shows/super-why
[6]https://pbskids.org/apps/super-why-app.html
[7]Their products are "Completely word-free. Based on a research-backed curriculum from MIT and Princeton. Built with girls in mind without pandering. Self-directed — no experience required." https://codespark.com/about

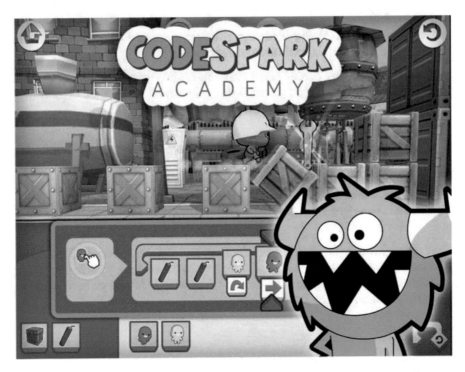

Figure 7-1. Meet one of the characters in the academy: The Glitch, who appears whenever there's a system error in Fooville. ©2021 codespark, Inc. All Rights Reserved

Jennifer manages a good section of the team and handles customer experience, which includes customer care as well as user testing, and the day-to-day needs of the production team.

One of the company's missions is to improve the gap in STEM education for underprivileged kids.[8]

Some of the questions about research with children that often come up in Jennifer's projects have changed over her career.

> It used to be, well, *What would we learn from testing with kids?*
>
> And it changed to *Well, we need to test with kids. How do we do it?*
>
> And even more recently it is *How do we get a sense of how kids are experiencing things when we can't actually interact with them in person?*

---

[8]https://codespark.com/

Tracking behavior and metrics as a conduit for insights

Jennifer is very aware of the biases associated with in-person testing and one of the ways she approaches this is through metrics:

> There's a bias that comes in when someone is being observed, because they know they're being observed. And since metrics are essentially invisible, it changes the lens through which we're able to observe behavior. And it's much more naturalistic and it creates a much more naturalistic environment than even sitting in the living room with the researcher observing. If you really want naturalistic behavior, you have to remove as much of the artificial framing as you can.'

Tracking data enables us to observe kids naturally having a digital experience with, say, a creative tool. We can see what they're doing, what's appealing to them without actually having to stop them to ask. Jennifer explains

> It's a window into the mind that we've never been able to have before. This is hard data that would have been impossible to collect about kids' play in the real world. How would you know how many times a child has played a Disney Tangled narrative – who would know if it was 1 time or 57 times over the last month? You couldn't do it, right? You couldn't do it. But today we could actually develop, in theory at least, a picture of everything a child has done on a device to very fine detail. For example if I've used this stamp in this creative tool 538 times or I have used that creative tool twice and this other creative tool with different IP in it or whatever 50 times. So the scale of information that we can gather is tremendous.

Jennifer links tracking as a potential solution to the problem of cognitive ability bias:

> I've spent my career working on early learning. And I haven't even touched learning for kids who are nonverbal. It's exponentially difficult for us as neurotypical adults to understand what a neuro-atypical child might be making of the play experience. The asymmetry in that relationship is so so big that it's really, really difficult to bridge that.

She points to a way to address this challenge:

> I'm thinking about the naturalism of the environment. Can we get them something that we can have them use as unobtrusively observed as possible? And metrics come into play again there. Obviously people have tried to use metrics in the way of having coding for video content, for example, researchers are often using that. To me, metrics is the next level of that, because it's actually hard numbers that are very precisely defined.

The significance of licenses of Intellectual Property (IP) in creative works and narratives is rising – and thus also in research

When Jennifer is involved in producing and designing a digital experience, many fundamental questions arise:

> I want to understand what is engaging about what we're doing. So is it the fact that there's music? Is it the fact that there's cute characters that they recognize? What are the elements that contribute to saliency from the kids perspective?

The term *salience*, a special area of attention, can help us understand the impact of brands and characters licensed from IP owners, such as Disney. Jennifer wonders exactly how important the saliency is, and how much she wants to rely on that in terms of facilitating the play experience in her product. She concludes that:

> Something is lost when you're using toys purely as a vehicle for telling – or in fact retelling – other people's stories. You're giving the kids a context, but how much of this narrative is already predetermined for the child?

> This raises many questions that research can help to answer:

> How is that predetermined narrative changing the child's imaginative play? Strong framing from a movie or a similar narrative could be positive and encourage the child to do something that he or she probably wouldn't do otherwise. But is it limiting? To me it brings up so many questions of what kids understand, how they understand it, and then how they put that understanding into play.

From a research perspective it can be a tricky task to separate the significance of the IP from the overall experience. But the question remains: will the digital experience be as engaging and attractive to the child if it does not include a well-known, relatable character? The challenge in studying a well-loved brand is that it has a positive aura or halo that overshadows other mechanics or aspects of the experience or product: "Oh, it's Barbie or LEGO Friends or *Frozen*. Then I'll love it" (if these are the brands the child resonates well with), or at least the experience will be perceived more positively than the same experience without the IP.

To Jennifer the significance of IP has progressed tremendously over the years, from a time in our shared past in the previous century when kids had few TV channels to choose from and large cinematic narratives happened only in... well, cinemas, and they were special occasions.

> I remember developing very elaborate play narratives as a kid, and I'm sure that that still happens. I'm not saying that it doesn't, but it has changed how children play and of course it's changed their narratives. I don't look at it as a good or a bad thing. I just think it is a kind of utter dominance of IP.

Including IP or not (and specifically with characters) is a very real dilemma for producers like Jennifer, as an IP is costly but perhaps represents the only way to get the child's attention. For a researcher it is also a dilemma to sort out which parts of the child's behavior, responses, and attitudes are IP specific and which are product specific. To what extent is the child having a good experience because she is interacting with Elsa from *Frozen* and to what extent is it because she enjoys the product? This is where A/B-testing (A being with one IP, B being with another) could provide some data.

Longitudinal research is more important than stakeholders think

When thinking about common stakeholder misconceptions of research with children, Jennifer points to the unrealistic expectation that kids will provide a definitive answer and guidance:

> Generally, I find that research with kids really just brings up more questions. You can obviously make some generalizations, but most often I feel like it just brings up more questions or more ideas. For stakeholders the most important thing to understand is it's a process that doesn't end. It doesn't have a

beginning point, and it doesn't have an ending point. One of the things that intrigues me most is longitudinal research, into what kids are doing over time.

She underscores the importance of understanding how play and the interaction with a product evolves over time. It is just as important as knowing whether it's an appealing box right off the shelf, as most often kids don't always have control over whether they get that box or not. Sure, they have pocket money and they can save up for something, but quite often things are gifts. She continues:

> What does that mean or entail to develop something for appeal over the next six months or two years? People of my generation still have all of our Lego from the first space sets that we had when we were kids. Will that be the case for the children of today?

"It's almost impossible to give kids enough time to respond"

Jennifer sees a potential drawback in more conventional in-person, moderated research:

> I think the number one thing that I've learned in research is it's almost impossible to give kids enough time to respond. It's so easy as adults to want to fill the space with talking. But kids haven't developed that easy ability with language yet. I think we do kids such a tremendous disservice by trying to talk to them while they're trying to play. You know play is their work and they don't even know what they're doing most of the time. So trying to ask them about it, it's such a wrong way of going about it, and that's why I'm so fascinated by metrics because it allows us to actually give kids the space to play. And space to do things and without that pressure of "somebody's watching me."

Jennifer points to another drawback of not giving kids enough time:

> Because kids get excited, that can be a false barometer of their understanding of what they're doing. Kids are excited by a shiny new thing, and they can be instantly attracted to something. But actually understanding how that thing is working for them takes a surprising amount of time.

She points to patience as a necessary virtue for a researcher:

> I need now to give them time to respond to me in their own way and not interrupt the way that we're so conditioned to do as adults to fill space. Kids don't have that conditioning.

▮ **Note** These biases are also discussed in Step 7 (…for the right duration) and Step 13 (Monitored by the right people) in Chapter 2.

Using research to make classrooms a better experience for students and teachers

Rasmus Horn works with user research and experience quality in LEGO Education and studies how products work in the classroom context. Before joining LEGO, Rasmus worked with global customer acceptance testing in the high-end audio company Bang & Olufsen, where I first met him.

LEGO Education offers classroom lessons covering all ages, from pre-Kindergarten to grade 12, and subjects across the STEAM spectrum from early language and literacy to coding and robotics[9]

One example of a product for the younger pre-K and Kindergarten kids is the 45025 Coding Express, which covers 8 lessons for 6 young students, where "early learners will learn through play about sequencing, looping, conditional coding, and cause and effect by placing the new action bricks within the train's track. Each action brick creates a specific action allowing for students to test and redesign ways to problem-solve and work together to get their train to its destination."[10]

Another example for the older students in grades 6–8 is the LEGO Education SPIKE Prime Set. It combines bricks and hardware, and a drag-and-drop coding language based on Scratch to "engage students through playful learning activities to think critically and solve complex problems, regardless of their learning level. From easy-entry projects to limitless creative design possibilities, SPIKE Prime helps students learn the essential STEAM[11] and 21st-century skills needed to become the innovative minds of tomorrow."[12]

---

[9] https://education.lego.com/en-us/lessons
[10] https://education.lego.com/en-us/products/coding-express-by-lego-education/45025#coding-express
[11] Where STEM represents science, technology, engineering and math, STEAM adds the arts – humanities, language arts, dance, drama, music, visual arts, design, and new media. To read more about STEAM and its predecessor STEM, go to https://theconversation.com/explainer-whats-the-difference-between-stem-and-steam-95713
[12] www.lego.com/en-us/product/lego-education-spike-prime-set-45678

Are the children reading or not?

Some of LEGO Education's products are for early learning in the gap between kindergarten and first, second, and third grades. This provides a challenge to Rasmus and his colleagues:

> That means that we have students that are reading and someone not reading and that makes us consider what happens in the learning context. So we have two different coding languages – one coding language with icon blocks and one with text blocks. One of the things that we're trying to figure out is what happens in that span? When do students move into using the text blocks? And when do they use the icon blocks and what do they do with it? What role does reading play?

Rasmus and his colleagues also use storytelling in some lessons. To get to that, the students need to read small snippets of texts or illustrations, which again raises the question of how children will interpret a storyline. To get a better understanding of this, Rasmus and his team observe the children and what they're doing. They have also been using eye tracking to see if the children are reading the texts or looking at illustrations:

> We can see that somewhere between six and seven years something happens and that's of course connected to their ability to read.

Is a lesson being learned or not?

Rasmus is also working on assessing various lessons they offer. He relies on the Learning-through-Play Framework by Garrett James Jaeger and his colleagues at the LEGO Foundation (discussed earlier in this chapter and in Chapter 1). It offers us a tool for assessing learning through play. They have so far been focusing on individual learning, but since Rasmus's audiences are working with classrooms, they are trying to modify the tool so that it can also assess how a lesson works in a classroom.

They have five areas that they're investigating:

1. How *fun* is a lesson? Because it's Lego, it has to be fun.

2. Is it *engaging*? One of the attributes of fun is that it engages.

3. Is it *meaningful*? This is the opposite of frustrating or confusing.

4. Is it *iterative*? Does it inspire students to go back and do it again, perhaps better or faster?

5. Is it *socially interactive*? How do students interact with each other during the learning experiences that we aim to provide?

These five areas are subject to measurement in a manner that reflects many of the intentions of the KX score discussed in Chapter 6:

> We are really trying to set it up as a quantitative assessment tool where you can end up with a score. I'd like to be able to benchmark lessons against each other, and so we're taking that tool to see if we can use that indication as a KPI, a Key Performance Indicator, as a measure of success for lessons, or figure out what lessons are good and what lessons are bad in the classroom, and what works well and what works not so well.

The independent set of eyes and ears

One of Rasmus's roles is to coordinate the testing process and collaborate with teachers and schools. He handles all the "footwork" around testing, setting it up so that designers and concept people can come into the classroom and observe. This comes with opportunities and challenges:

> I'm the independent set of eyes and ears, not governed or influenced by the rest of the team. I'm not a part of any of the design teams. I'm a testing resource. And so hopefully I can have no bias, maybe I should say another bias, because there is always a bias somewhere. There are the ones that we are aware of and the ones that we are not aware of, but at least I am just a fresh pair of eyes on what we're testing.
>
> So it's my role to try and find the right questions to ask. What is it that we're looking for? Some designers have a tendency to ask a lot of questions during a session and have too many things to observe at one time. It will obstruct the intended outcome of the test. Sometimes it's better to have several tests with a very narrow focus and trying to be really sharp. "What is it that we're looking for *this time*?" It also points to future testing.

Specifically when it comes to reporting findings to designers, Rasmus says:

> If designers are not present during the sessions, and I come back to designers, they will have a lot of questions – what did the kids say to this, or what they did say to that? Eight out of ten times I do not really have an answer. Because what the designers may ask about was not the focus of the tests. Sometimes it is better just to have a very limited but very precise answer than one that's fairly broad and up to discussion. This is not to say that it should be the only testing approach though.

How can we take the fun out of the equation and simply measure learning?

Rasmus and his colleagues have a specific issue to face, since children are generally very happy to be playing with Lego during school hours: how do we study the product and its potential pain points and find out what it is that we can make better? This is specific to a school setting, because normal schoolwork is often seen as boring and tedious. He has a solution to this problem:

> As soon as the teacher brings in Lego, it's almost no matter what the students are doing, they're just happy because they get to play with Lego. As researchers we really have to look through that joy of playing in the school and them getting to play. Instead, we'll be looking at how many questions the students ask and how busy is the teacher at running around providing guidance and solutions?

> We have one metric being how many questions they ask and another being if they are self-lead: how many times do the students ask the teacher? What is the type of questions? Is it because they're stuck? That they do not know what to do? That is another metric.

> The time spent, especially the building time, is something we measure. Students are enjoying building even though it takes 30 minutes to build something. But this is not necessarily good, because the class session is only 45 minutes, so we have to spend only maybe 10 or 15 minutes building. But what if it takes them 20 minutes? The students could still score it at 10 out of 10 smileys because it was fun, but they did

not get to the learning portion or only part of it. They did not have time to experiment and to learn. The purpose is — and that's what makes the teacher happy — to get to the a-ha moments where learning is taking place. For us, the Lego Foundation framework has really been helpful in putting words to what that moment is and what the learning process consists of. For instance, one level of outcome is that a child can own an experience. That's one of the highest levels. But the next one is transferring, being able to put a skill or knowledge or experience into a new area. To see students go from one level to another, that's what we like.

Do we pay students, schools, or teachers for their help in our research? And how?

A very practical question in much research is how to incentivize or remunerate our respondents. In Rasmus's case, would it mean paying the children, the schools, or the teachers? Regarding public employees, in most countries they are not allowed to receive gifts or any kind of payments. Often it is a question of how to say "Thank you for your help and your time." Rasmus has a solution for this:

> What we do is that we will never pay the teachers. We also do not give gifts to the students in the schools, because that can be seen as marketing. So we're very cautious about that. But we do pay the school itself for renting their teachers time, and also for rental of rooms. If we take a classroom for a full day, we'll pay for the rent. And then it's not gifts, it's simply just payment for a service.
>
> It depends on how much time we need. Sometimes we just want the teacher to do what they would have done anyway without us being there, and we're asking them not to change their plans to accommodate us in doing specific lessons for our sake. It's another question if we ask them to deviate from what they would have done by themselves and spend more time to prepare this. Ultimately the school issues an invoice to us for the time that teachers have spent.

Presenting and sustaining findings – taking research seriously

Some big questions that most researchers struggle with is how to present results and how to make sure that actions are taken on the research findings. Usually we will resort to writing findings in a report and presenting them to the team. Most often this just happens one time, and then the report is stored and no one will look at it ever again. So the question is, how do we make sure that the action points are agreed upon and that someone owns them after that? Rasmus knows this challenge very well and he offers a solution and an example:

> It could all be wasted work, and the project will just continue regardless because of their timelines and the deadlines they have to live up to. We want to be making sure that we get the most impact out of the effort that we've done in the research. One way to do that is simply by creating a task, documenting that we have a problem and then assigning it to someone: you are now the owner of this, how would you mitigate this? How will you make sure we do not do this again in the future, e.g. in the next product if it's too late to do something in this one? If we can change it, then we need to make sure there is a corrective action or a plan for solving it. One thing that we are working on is visualizing the number of issues that we still have open.

> For example if we found some problems with the Bluetooth connection flow in a prototype test in the spring of 2019, and now here, a year after, we can hear it as a complaint from the market. And that's when it comes in handy that we can go back and say, well, we created this issue already a year ago. Because the product was under time pressure, they didn't solve it at that time. So now we have the problem in the market. So we can go back and say, well, research actually found it a year ago, but there wasn't any action being taken. And that's a strong argument to take research seriously. There is a reason that it's a pain point, and we can be sure that we will hear about it when the product is in the market. That's also sharpening our research because we know, OK, maybe we should have been even more clear in our messaging back then. Our system will need to be able to store issues in a way so it's not just sitting in reports that we forget about.

When external researchers leave, so do their insights. Will it leave a vacuum of accountability?

Another question that comes up in research is the use of external consultants. This poses a challenge that Rasmus has firsthand experience with, and he points to organizing around it as a solution:

> It comes down to being able to hold people accountable. An external researcher or an external research company has come in, delivered a result, they deliver the report and then they're out. There's no one holding the project accountable. We need a mechanism that says "So we found this issue, what have you done about it? What are the actions?" There needs to be a stakeholder holding the organization accountable for the things that we found in research. Externals do not have the same position or power to come back and say "Well, I found this issue in our tests, why haven't you fixed it?" There needs to be someone representing the voice of the customer and being the users' stakeholder or advocate in projects. That provides a mandate.

Research with children in a public service concept development context

Camilla Balslev Nielsen holds a PhD in Children's Play Culture and Technology from the University of Aarhus and a Master in Design, Communication, and Media with a focus on children and their digital culture. She works at the Danish Broadcasting Corporation (DR) and is heading up the Danish digital learning project called ultra:bit.[13] The aim of ultra:bit is to inspire children from 8 to 14 years old (4th to 8th graders) not only to be major consumers of technology but to be creators of technology. At the same time, the project urges the kids to take on a critical position to the technology in our surroundings. ultra:bit is developed by DR in close cooperation with CFU (the Teachers Resource Center) and Astra (the National Center for Science Education). It is supported by the Danish Industry Foundation, and more than 30 partners are contributing to the project. It was originally inspired by the BBC and the Micro:bit Educational Foundation.

---

[13]www.dr.dk/om-dr/ultrabit (in Danish) – related to the British Micro:bit: https://microbit.org/ (in English). The ultra:bit box is produced by DR Commercial and over 100,000 micro:bits have been distributed to the 1300 schools (8 out of 10) in Denmark, who are involved in the project.

The project is quite successful as the proportion of Danish 6th graders who say that they can code increased from 27% (2018) to 78% (2020).[14] Camilla was my colleague when she worked for LEGO in campaign and content strategy, and before that she also had children and teens as her target group when she worked as Digital Business Developer in Egmont, a large media company in the Nordic region.

A public service media institution has — in many of the same ways as a commercial business does — tasks and challenges that lead to a profound need for research. Camilla says

> It is important that we continue to produce different kinds of high-quality content and activities which are adjusted and based on children's everyday life in Denmark. First of all, to create an alternative to what they see on e.g. YouTube but also to make sure that it fits a Danish context. Today there is so much other content around them, and in order to come up with relevant content and activities for children, you need to understand what drives them.

Research plays an important role in a complex and ambitious multi-stakeholder project like ultra:bit, which is developed by DR in close cooperation with more than 30 partners. Camilla's role is to secure and develop the collaboration between the different internal and external project partners who deliver courses for teachers, TV programs, teaching materials, and STEM conferences. But she also plays an important role in creating the concepts around activities and content for children who are between 8 and 14 years old. It's about giving them some tools so instead of just being users of technology, they can also be creative with technologies. Together with her colleagues she has set up the interactive online learning event "ultra:bit LIVE" for more than 15,000 children in Denmark, which includes a national innovation contest.

Since these concepts are mostly used in schools, they need to meet the specific requirements from the government, but it is also important that they align with the broadcaster's (DR's) own way of creating quality content for children. The concepts and topics also need to be fun, engaging, and inviting to the children — not too hard, overwhelming, or too boring, but rather something that they can cope with and which they find relevant.

---

[14]www.dr.dk/om-dr/ultrabit/aargang-ultrabit-har-laert-kode (in Danish)

How to come up with concepts that are engaging to children

In order to align these many project requirements, Camilla researched the scope and the topics with children and also contacted the children's helpline (Børnetelefonen), a national initiative by the Danish NGO Children's Rights (Børns Vilkår), that since 1987 offers anonymous counselling and guidance to children. With them Camilla was able to take a closer look at those topics that children are concerned or worried about, such as bullying, divorces, abuse, a life with digital media, depression, and loneliness, as well as climate change and how children could help adults reduce climate change – which became the theme for 2019.

> At the beginning of the concept phase, I research specific topics and here at this stage it is important for me to find some insights that can be the concept's "why?" – the underlying justification that can bring all the stakeholders together. In this case we found out that climate changes are something that occupy children and after talking with both children and parents we also learned that children often educate their parents about how they can act better in their everyday life to reduce the climate changes.
>
> And then I test the concept with target groups, which in this case are teachers and students. I also test the concept with other people around the children, such as politicians or people working in different organizations that are important to the children.
>
> It is very important to know what children prefer *now* and *why* and one of the ways to tap into that is through influencers. I need to follow what is interesting for the children and see if I can maybe create concepts around those topics that they can relate to.

Camilla describes her general approach, which to me is immersive and personally involved, and points to the benefits of a hands-on approach to research:

> I try to stay curious and I think that's one of the most important ingredients when you work with children and you want to know what is important for them. You also need to be playful and you also need to try it out. So if they are following someone on, let's say Instagram, then I'll do the same thing. If they're using TikTok, I'm trying to see what they do on TikTok. If they're playing

certain games – for instance right now they're playing Among us – then I'll try to figure out what that is. Even though I might not be very good at it, I'm still trying to play and to find some children who want to play with me. I get my information when I talk to the children, I need to try it out, and then I ask a lot of questions.

One of the many personal benefits or perks of being an adult researcher with children as the target group is that you learn a great deal from the children, and you learn it in many different areas. Camilla mentions a few examples:

It is amazing how willing to try out new things children are compared to us adults. I also think that it is really cool to see how the children explore technology. When you compare the way I am using a mobile phone to them, then I'm using more steps, but for them it's also about optimizing their steps. They only want to click once, but for me, I just found a way that works and will stick with it, but they think in a different way. They don't want to waste time. We have different expectations to and ways of approaching technology.

Sometimes they have a problem and can come up with solutions that I would have never thought about. For example I like to watch Netflix series while I cook and that usually works well but then I started a series in Spanish, *La casa de papel,*[15] and since I don't understand Spanish I had to constantly look at the screen and the subtitles. But then my youngest son said "You can just just choose English voice over" and I was like "What!" I thought I could only change the subtitles.

That is a great example because they are growing up with more global content then I was and they expect it to fit them, but they are also ready to make an effort to adjust to it. They learn e.g. English while playing games or watching YouTube and some of the streaming services. We also learned to be able to play and learned through play so looking at children today you can say "everything and nothing" has changed. Children's interaction with technology is complex and not a black box. There is a need for doing research about the relations between humans and non-humans in different contexts if you want to understand it.

---

[15]which translates directly into *The Paper House*, but in English it is called *Money Heist*, https://en.wikipedia.org/wiki/Money_Heist

Keeping an eye on the context and maintaining an open mind are key in research

Camilla is keenly aware of the significance of the context of her studies and how important it is to include the same children but in different contexts in order to gain a richer understanding.

> For instance, how they use the mobile phone in one way when they are on transportation and then it's just different when they are together with the football guys or when they are at school or if they are at home. So you need to be mindful of how that context shapes the mood of the child, maybe their intentions: maybe the child wants to behave politely when the child is with parents, but not so much with friends. As a researcher, you should sometimes try and let them do their own thing as much as possible.
>
> You have to stay open-minded to what is happening when you get out into the field. My PhD was about girls and technology, and when I got out there in the field and I was doing observational studies amongst girls, I found out that, well, the girls are not playing only with girls and technology. They are also playing with boys. So yes, it's very important that ahead of the study you have some sort of understanding of the kids and the subject that you want to research, but when you come out into the field, you have to be ready to throw it away and be open-minded and ready to see what is really going on. Otherwise, you won't get it. I mean, it can be a waste of time. Your plans are only good until the moment you actually meet the kids.
>
> But that's also a good part about doing research. Something new always comes up and you go "Really!? Ahh, is this what it is like?" It can also be quite funny. I did a research project with children about their toys and invited children to take pictures of for instance their toys at home.
>
> We talked about the pictures and they told me that some of the toys they don't play with but when I asked why it was still in their rooms, they told me because they played with it. They would just not bring the toys to school and only play with it alone or with a good friend. A toy's lifetime extends over several phases

and they can be attached to it in different ways. The combination of research methods made it possible for me to learn more about the relations between children and toys.

Children are not simply the victims of technology

In the first chapter of this book I highlighted the status of children in society and how this status affects research, and I discussed how adults will miss out on many insights if they only see children as passive recipients and users of media and technology. This is also an issue close to Camilla's heart.

> If you really dive into what children are doing with technology, as I did in my PhD and have continued to do in my work, then you will start to see that oftentimes they are in fact controlling it and it's not always the other way around. In the beginning when they get started with something new, the game-design is hidden for them. A part of the play culture is to ask and help each other to investigate the design to first relive it and then redesign it so it fits their needs and wishes. If they e.g. want to get a specific character which is randomly chosen by the game – then at one point – they are like "Yeah, I can hit the reset button." So that's one thing.

> But I also think it's very important that we don't think that children know everything about technology and leave them alone. And especially now, because with all the available data and Machine Learning,[16] I think it's very important that we are aware of how we in our society can support the children to also be critical towards the technology around them. Technology is playing a bigger part in their lives than in previous generations, and as a concept developer or researcher you need to try to be balanced in your perspective of them. They shouldn't be victimized, but on the other hand, they shouldn't be left alone.

> Technology is changing rapidly and changing our ways of interacting with each other. There is a need for adults who are curious and interested together with the children.

---

[16]Machine learning (ML) is the study of computer algorithms that improve automatically through experience – see https://en.wikipedia.org/wiki/Machine_learning

The children may not worry about how their data is collected or stored and what can happen afterwards. When you produce and research with children it is complex. It is therefore positive that ultra:bit as one initiative in Denmark can support teachers and students to experiment with technology by a playful learning approach.

This ties very well into Samantha Punch's school of thought as to children's role in society (see Chapter 1).

Innovation through research with children

Nanna Borum is Senior Design Researcher at LEGO's Creative Play Lab in Denmark and works at the very forefront of product and play innovation as part of a team called Innovation, Foresight, Strategy, and Culture.

Some examples of the products produced by Nanna's team are the Hidden Side (2019),[17] which brought augmented reality, a mobile game, and physical play experiences together in a scary haunted house type story, as well as LEGO Super Mario (2020),[18] which, in collaboration with Nintendo, captures the charm and characters of the original video game while adding in a lot of building and playing.

In the Hidden Side story, children can experience a haunted version of reality by using an app. The augmented reality is activated when the app detects certain digital cues from the physical sets. This means that children can play with the physical set alone, or with the app alone, or with both.

The LEGO Super Mario product line has a Starter Course and several expansion sets, of which two are the "Boomer Bill Barrage" and the "Piranha Plant Power Slide."

Co-creating new products and new ways of playing – with an emphasis on co-

Her team is focused on developing new play themes, products, and characters rather than on continuing the development of already-successful product lines such as LEGO Friends (2012)[19] or LEGO City (1978).[20] This puts Nanna at the very forefront of product innovation and even business disruption in

---

[17]www.lego.com/en-us/themes/hidden-side/about
[18]www.lego.com/en-us/themes/super-mario/about
[19]https://en.wikipedia.org/wiki/Lego_Friends
[20]https://en.wikipedia.org/wiki/Lego_City

LEGO, which demonstrates that research can be instrumental in innovation and disruption – two paradigms that are crucial to most businesses.

The way her team is organized gives her a unique role as a researcher. Nanna's role is to help the teams stay at eye level with the children during the development of new products, and she most often participates in projects during the very early exploratory phase of innovation development as a "full-blown qualitative researcher":

> My role is to be part of the team. I'm not a plug-in researcher. I'm always part of the project team and the development team and I take part in all the daily meetings. I am part of the core team and I help shape and support and push and provoke the teams in making sure that the kids are at the center of our design.

Working as a "plug-in researcher" myself, I am sometimes envious of a role like Nanna's, since it allows her to follow the development of a product over many months, sometimes years, and to dive into the details of that product's reception and its audience. In some cases she works on projects where there's no actual product yet or where the focus is not the product:

Right now I'm working on two different projects with two different target groups. I have a project that's aimed towards a specific target group with specific needs and I have another project that is aimed towards more value-based play. It's two completely different ways into understanding our users, and it's also two different ways of testing. In the project that's very value-based, we really have to dig deep and get an understanding of what's driving and motivating our users. The focus is actually not so much on the actual product – we use the product to understand their values, to have something to talk around when it comes to understanding their values. The other project that is aimed towards a specific target group with specific needs is way later in the process, and we're at a point now where we're doing very concrete, specific concept testing and using different methodologies for that.

Innovation requires dedicated researchers

Nanna sees some distinct advantages of having a dedicated researcher in an innovation team, since it can sometimes be a challenge for a project team to keep the focus on the children rather than on a great idea or on some great new technology:

> When we work in the project teams, everybody is passionate and everybody is super skilled, super motivated. But everybody also most often has a key competence and it's something that they are to some

extent a bit geeky about also. When we get to a place where everybody is combining all their geekiness, we make awesome products right? But it's sometimes easier to see your own objectives or your own development first, and you'll have your own idea about what a great experience is. This of course depends on who's in the team and it's very different from team to team. I do think that a lot of our designers are excellent at keeping the kids' needs and experiences within eyesight at all times. But then sometimes they just get passionate, and then it can get lost a bit in translation from us to the child. So that's where I come in to just help translate some of the trends and facts about what it really means for a child and to help shape the design guidelines, encompassing all the different aspects of the children's experience. Whether it's how well an 8 year-old can read or whether it's if a four year old can do so-and–so with their hands. It's necessary sometimes for a project to remain relevant to just be very, very close to the children and make sure that the designers understand exactly what a child is able to do and exactly what are they driven by, and exactly what is moving in the children's culture right now.

Understanding needs – also primordial needs – is a driver for innovation

Innovation in a company such as LEGO involves many competencies and areas of expertise, ranging from the compounds that go into the bricks, to the molds that produce them, to the specific bricks and how they are compiled into a model. Innovation also includes how that model can be brought to life in play and how it can spark stories and ignite imagination in the child that will ultimately play with it. This is Nanna's field of work.

> My focus is on the experience more than, say, the physical model itself or its stability. I'm looking at questions like: Where are the small play starters? Where are the story starters in the model, and what is it really that makes this into an experience? I also touch a bit upon the communication in order to design a holistic experience.

We most often start from scratch, with either no brief at all or with a very vague brief. Most often we start in what we call an opportunity space that can be shaped by either trends we see in society or some primordial needs that we are not currently addressing with our product portfolio.

For instance, the product line Hidden Side worked with scariness. As a feeling, being scared is ingrained in people from a very young age and helps humans to be careful and cautious around uncertainties in the environment. It may seem like a far stretch and a rare endeavor for a toy manufacturer to deliberately produce a scary toy, but the toy market and children's play have a surprising number of scary dolls, zombies, animals (fictitious or real) with scary attributes, scary sounds and locations, or simply games that are played at night or in a darkened room. As in many other aspects of design, the devil is in the detail – in getting it scary enough for the intended age group but not too scary, and this was the case with the Hidden Side.

We start by doing some kind of basic foundational research to understand the space. In that process we also start to understand what's driving the kids in the space we're striving to cover. There may also be parents in the space. We'll ask ourselves questions such as: What are the drivers in this space and what are the barriers? What are the needs that we can tap into? When we better understand what needs are out there, we also try to understand how are those needs not yet met? And then that's basically laying the foundation for our work when we are starting to shape the experience.

The Hidden Side had to be a little scary for the 8–10-year-olds. Scary can be good. In the Hidden Side we've aimed at designing an Augmented Reality (AR) game for mobile phones and we came up with a way to combine scariness with a functionality suitable to the AR experience. It can be challenging to design AR because with their mobile, the children can move the screen in any direction and the game has to make sense as much as possible, whether they point it upwards or downwards or to the side. The solution was ghosts simply because ghosts are not attached to the ground and they can be scary! It was a very practical thing – ghosts are hovering. That worked well in the story.

Research helps in many steps of the innovation and development process

Some organizations may rely on technological inventions or creative geniuses to drive their innovation process, but at LEGO the audience is very much in the center of the process, as Nanna explains, using Hidden Side as an example.

> We did quite a lot of research with the kids, where we made a scariness scale, and we took all kinds of different products for children that have a sense of scariness in them. Casper the friendly ghost. Scooby-doo. Urban legends like Slender Man.[21] In setting up the research we had conversations with the parents before they and their children joined, carefully telling them about what our intentions were. "This is what we're going to do with your children: They're going to discuss with us what is scary."

> We brought printed pictures of all the different scary products and then kids would rank them. Then they would tell us why it's scary or why it's definitely not scary. We did that for quite a lot of sessions to understand precisely where we are hitting the needle, because we wanted to make sure that it's scary enough to lure the older kids in, but it's also not too scary to scare away the six year old. So it was a very delicate balance we had to hit. One thing we figured out from that research was that what is actually scary – and this was especially true for kids in the younger end of that age group – is the unknown, say, when it's something that they cannot see or read or understand. Then it becomes scary. That informed our design – to focus more on *the unknown* and less on other aspects such as, for instance, the tone of voice.

---

[21]Slender Man is often depicted as a thin, unnaturally tall humanoid with a featureless head and face, wearing a black suit. Stories of the Slender Man commonly feature him stalking, abducting, or traumatizing people, particularly children. Source: https://en.wikipedia.org/wiki/Slender_Man

Toy reviews, YouTube style

Nanna has a rich arsenal of research methods. Here are two approaches that bring the peer-to-peer language of the children into the design process:

> One of the ways we tested was to ask children to make a toy review. With a phone in their hand, they were filming themselves while they were unfolding the functions in the app prototype on that phone. It informed us about their ability to hold the phone and navigate the functions at the same time. But it was also really an amazing source of data of how they understood the play and the models themselves, so I've actually been using that approach for other projects later on.
>
> It's very closely related to another method that we use, where we ask children to produce a peer review, where one kid is telling the others what the experience is about. And that's exactly what they do when they make a YouTube video. It makes them immediately tap into the language that they hear on YouTube and for us to hear that can provide really relevant data.

Qualitative research is very valuable at the beginning of a process

Some stakeholders in innovation and product development are quantitatively inclined and have the perception that lots of participants must mean a lot of data. This is not necessarily Nanna's experience when it comes to the exploration phase:

> We need different research for different periods in our development phases, and what I do is design research, and what we do in our department is everything before the validation process starts. So we spend most of our time exploring what a concept and experience can be. To make great experiences we truly need to understand our consumers, and I'm fully aware that people understand people differently. In my experience, when we are in a concept development phase of the project, seeing people with your concept in their hands and talking with them yourself will inspire and spark the concept development way more than numbers will.

Then when we move further down and into the development process, we need to validate if we actually have a consumer base for this project. Do we have the necessary amount of purchase intent? Do we have behavior that shows that people will buy into this concept?

Research impact can come in many different ways

Earlier in this book I covered the aspects of bias when moderating research sessions. In Nanna's projects, the researcher may likely be the one in a design team with the most research experience (and thus the most bias-aware) but shouldn't necessarily be the one moderating every session.

> I spend quite a lot of time and energy making sure that I'm not always the person in our team moderating. I'm not the researcher in the team, we're all researchers in the team. What I can do is the management and administration. I can set up everything, I can make sure we get the kids and parents in, or that we go out and visit parents and kids, but I will not be the one doing all the talking. I want the designers to talk with consumers directly themselves and make sure that I'm not just filtering their voices to them. In the teams where we do that it's working really nicely.
>
> Every team member has to just get over the hurdle that research takes time and it perhaps was easier just to get 10 key takeaways from a researcher. But after being through a process, the designers expressed that they truly enjoy spending time with consumers also. So it's not that they didn't want to. Actually they do really want to. It's just not their first thought. So you can try to manage it for them and make it easy and set it all up for them. But then you detract yourself in terms of the role as a moderator.

This marks a splendid opportunity to end this section with input from the experienced researchers. We have come to the final chapter of this book.

Summary

Finally, this chapter is a quick recap and a look at the bigger picture.

If we want kids to use our products or services…

…we will benefit tremendously from including children in the entire design process, from initial idea to after it has been launched, because

- Our stakeholders will be better aligned with the children's needs and wants.

- Our product will be more successful, as it has been designed with a focus on children's wants and needs.

- We'll suffer fewer and smaller costly setbacks in the process: there will be less moving backward in order to correct things that don't work.

- We'll have lower cost after launch to teach and train our support staff and users in how to use or understand the product, and we'll have less need for instructions, manuals, and consumer support.

Oh, and the kids will also benefit more from having a product or service that is more fun and more intuitive.

© Thomas Visby Snitker 2021
T. V. Snitker, *User Research with Kids*, https://doi.org/10.1007/978-1-4842-7071-4_8

User research is not rocket science...

...and there are straightforward techniques – tried and true in the UX research school of thought – that one can apply to every step of the process from beginning to end, such as

- Interviewing and observing, cultural probes, desk research
- Co-creation, testing sketches, wireframes, and prototypes
- Heuristic evaluations, formal and informal usability tests, in-person or remotely
- Ongoing measurement and testing

Rocket science should be left to... well, rocket scientists. But user research with children is a very accessible field. In fact, I believe that the more diverse the researchers and backgrounds on any project, the richer and fuller the representation of the children's experience that can be obtained, and as a result, the better the final outcome.

Yes, it requires rigor and a research mindset. Yes, it gets better as the researchers acquire more experience over time. And yes, compliance to legislation and best practice is a must.

But the point here, and throughout this book, is that these requirements and challenges to research with children must not deter us. People who come into this field with an interest but no experience should be encouraged to continue, perhaps by starting small, by iterating, and definitely by sharing their ideas and experiences. The world needs more research with children, not less.

Yes, there's bias everywhere, but...

...despair not! Humankind has survived so far not in spite of our biases, but rather *because of* them. Our biases allow us to make quick and generalized decisions ("There's a tiger. Better run."), and if these decisions were wrong ("Oh, the tiger also runs!"), well, we may still have time to make new ones before the tiger catches us (perhaps by climbing up a tree).

Our main concern as researchers is to be aware of these biases and consider ways to reduce their negative effects, whether it is

- Bias *before* the study, for example, if the objective or procedure is unclear
- Bias *during* the study, for example, if the setup or moderation is confusing to the participants
- Bias *after* the study, for example, if those at the receiving end of the findings misunderstand the results

Pre-study bias

In-study bias

Post-study bias

Figure 8-1. The bias chain demonstrated all the many ways that research bias (the little red stars) affects its target

Make the bias chain work for − not against − you

If you work in a role where you often create or respond to new research needs (e.g., by promoting or being part of a customer-centric culture in your organization), having a clear research process can save a lot of time and increase your profitability (Figure 8-1). This process should include everything from the intake of new projects (with criteria for accepting, rejecting, or postponing new research projects) to after the findings have been reported (with a road map for sustaining the findings and for verifying their implementation and effects).

The 18 steps to (not) ruining good research in Chapter 2 can serve as a blueprint for this process, as I show here:

18 steps to (not) ruining good research	Questions one could ask
1 For the right stakeholders or client	• Would you, dear stakeholders, be able to act upon the outcome of this study? How? • What means (e.g., fiscal, organizational, time, design) would you have at your disposal with which to act upon the findings? Are those means sufficient? • Is there another, similar research effort being carried out, perhaps one that would be able to have a bigger impact, e.g., due a larger scope or stronger decision-making power? • Have you established the most rewarding cost/benefit ratio between the study and its potential outcome? • Are the stakeholders' needs well aligned with their wants? Or do they actually need a different approach or scope than what they request?
2 The right objective or problem or pain	• Who has the pain and how serious is it? Why has it not been addressed before? • Is this the *most* painful pain? Will it go away by itself eventually? How soon? • Will the outcome of a study have business impact? • Does the study have the time and budget to make sufficient impact? • Who will care about the outcome?
3 The right product or project	• Why are we choosing to study this product? • Will we study the user experience of the product on its own, or in a larger context (e.g., to what degree are other products or services part of the job to be done)? • Which parts of the product will the study encompass (if not all the parts)? • If we leave out parts of the product in this study, will those parts be covered at a later point? • Is this scope relevant to all of the stakeholders? If we change the scope, can we then increase the relevancy and/or include more stakeholders?

(continued)

18 steps to (not) ruining good research	Questions one could ask
4 The right respondents, described in the right terms	• Who (which parts of the audience) will be included in the research project, and who will be left out? • Who in our organization should make this decision, and what are the criteria for inclusion and exclusion? • Are we using the right terms to describe the audience? Do we, for instance, use the same terms as the audience themselves do? • If we use age or gender as recruitment criteria, do we know if those criteria fit the actual audience or only the intended audience? Would it be more meaningful to use skill level (whether platform and/or service) or interest areas as recruitment criteria? • Can we make sure that we recruit children who actually feel that they belong to the target group (as opposed to their parents imagining so)?
5 Doing the right things	• Will the children in the study be doing something that they find relevant? • Have we determined what "the right things to do" are (and are not)? • Is there a fair overlap between the purpose of the study and what the children feel are "the right things" to do? And is there a shared expectation about the sequence and duration of events between the study and the respondents?
6 …at the right time of day or week or month	• Will the study happen at a convenient time for the children? • Has the timing been chosen to accommodate the children's schedule (as opposed to the researcher's or stakeholder's)? • What influence could the chosen time of day or week potentially have on the outcome of the study?
7 …for the right duration	• Will the duration of the study be convenient for the children? • Has the duration been chosen to accommodate the children's schedule and abilities (as opposed to the researcher's or stakeholder's)? • What influence could the chosen duration potentially have on the outcome of the study?
8 …in the right location/setting	• Will the study happen at a convenient, safe, and comfortable location for the children? • Has the location been chosen to accommodate the children's schedule (as opposed to the researcher's or stakeholder's)? • If several children participate, are we aware of how they feel about each other, and how their relationships may affect the study? • What influence could the chosen location potentially have on the outcome of the study? Will it, for instance, deliver a better-than-real experience?

(continued)

18 steps to (not) ruining good research	Questions one could ask
9 …using the right device	• Is the chosen device one that children are comfortable and/or experienced with? How will their skill level influence their experience or performance during the study?
10 Correctly primed and instructed	• Do we make sure that the respondents understand the purpose of the study and what they are expected to do? • Are we mindful of all the (more or less subtle) ways that we will be influencing (priming and instructing) a child throughout the process of participating in our study? And how can we reduce their stress, performance anxiety, and insecurity? • Do we use age-appropriate language and artifacts to minimize talking up or down to the child?
11 The right amount of priming and instruction	• Can we design the session with respect to the amount of verbal dialogue and chatter so that the session resembles the real usage context? • How can we make sure that we provide the children enough time to experience the product, to think about it, and to express themselves?
12 Correctly moderated	• Do we need moderation, and if so, what qualifications do moderators need to have? If parents are the moderators (e.g., in remote sessions), how do we equip them for the task? • Are we being conscious of the physical influences on the session, such as our clothes, tone, and body language? And of the verbal influences, such as asking neutral, simple, clear, and concrete questions to reduce misunderstanding? • Are we mindful of the order of questions, e.g., asking general questions before specific questions, open questions before closed questions, and behavior questions before attitude questions (to name a few examples)? • Can we help the moderators to mimic the child's energy level (e.g., not being too boisterous or too mellow)?
13 Monitored by the right people	• How can we encourage relevant observers to join? • And how can we ensure that they get the most relevant observations possible? • How do we manage observers and their expectations (for instance, through a written code of conduct)?

(continued)

18 steps to (not) ruining good research	Questions one could ask
14 A rigorous, methodical analysis	• How can we ensure that our researchers apply analytical and critical thinking skills, and that they identify common themes, patterns, and relationships within the behavior and responses of the respondent group? • Can we tell a good analysis from a bad analysis?
15 A timely, relevant, and actionable report	• Do we know who needs to see the report, and what their interests and competencies are? Is there a deadline for their attention? • How do we increase the likelihood that the stakeholders read the report (whether written, spoken, presented as a movie, or given in some other format)?
16 A simple and focused presentation	• What constitutes a successful presentation in this particular case? • Is a presentation a suitable format to communicate the findings? Or to put it another way, given the findings and the stakeholders, what would be the best way to present to them?
17 Sustaining the findings	• The researcher has handed over and shared the results and they now live on, perhaps travelling from one person to the next. In Chapter 2, I used the Chinese whisper game as a metaphor for this process. The results may fade from everyone's memory, or perhaps they'll be misconstrued along the way. This begs an answer to the following question. • Will the findings need to be made present again at a later point, and if so, when, how, and to whom should they be presented? Who will be responsible for this?
18 Actioned right	• We've arrived at the million-dollar question: Will the research lead to anything? • How do we make sure that those who *can* do something (e.g., a designer or a developer), *will* do something? • Will that *something* be in accordance with the research findings? • Is this a good time for the project to discuss the next research initiative?

The joy, delight, and beauty of research with children

As I mentioned at the beginning of this book, one challenge for the adult researchers is to put themselves in the child's place, to walk in their shoes so to speak, because they cannot unlearn all the skills that they have acquired on the road into adulthood. But it seems very fitting to mention here at the end of the book how rewarding taking that challenge is. Although this book has focused on the perils and pitfalls of research with children, I find it imperative to stress how delightful it is. This is echoed in my interviews with experts mentioned earlier. As Jennifer Wells has said

> The way children's brains work is constantly surprising, and they'll take something and turn it completely on its head. I love it. And I love hearing them talk about where their flights of fancy are going, because it's so unpredictable and inspiring.

When talking to practitioners, I often hear researchers talk about the joy they take in the firsthand encounters with children. Being a researcher with children as the audience is a profession and a way to earn a living, but also a constant reminder to the researcher about human experiences in general and children's experiences in particular, and about how important it is for adults – researchers, but also designers, producers, marketers, decision-makers, and others – to do their best and to take children and their needs and experiences seriously.

Index

© Thomas Visby Snitker 2021

T. V. Snitker, *User Research with Kids*, https://doi.org/10.1007/978-1-4842-7071-4

Printed in the United States
by Baker & Taylor Publisher Services